The Immutable Laws of Living

the
IMMUTABLE LAWS
of
Living

*The Inspirational
Blueprint to Living
Your Meaningful Life*

Lee H. Baucom, Ph.D.

NEW YORK

LONDON • NASHVILLE • MELBOURNE • VANCOUVER

The Immutable Laws of Living

The Inspirational Blueprint to Living Your Meaningful Life

Published in New York, New York, by Morgan James Publishing. Morgan James is a trademark of Morgan James, LLC. www.MorganJamesPublishing.com

The Morgan James Speakers Group can bring authors to your live event. For more information or to book an event visit The Morgan James Speakers Group at www.TheMorganJamesSpeakersGroup.com.

ISBN 9781683506898 paperback
ISBN 9781683506904 eBook
Library of Congress Control Number: 2017911835

Cover Design by:
Rachel Lopez
www.r2cdesign.com

Interior Design by:
Chris Treccani
www.3dogcreative.net

In an effort to support local communities, raise awareness and funds, Morgan James Publishing donates a percentage of all book sales for the life of each book to Habitat for Humanity Peninsula and Greater Williamsburg.

Get involved today! Visit
www.MorganJamesBuilds.com

For Kathy, my partner and supporter through the journey of life. Thank you for walking with me through this interesting path of life!

TABLE OF CONTENTS

INTRODUCTION

Accccording to the handy-dandy online dictionary, immutable means "unchanging over time or unable to be changed." So an immutable law is one that doesn't change over time. You can't change it, and I can't change it. We can choose to obey it, or we can choose to disobey it, but only at our own expense.

In the natural world, we are surrounded by immutable laws every day. For example, there is the immutable law of gravity. It is irrelevant whether you believe in gravity or not; gravity acts upon you at all times. I can attest to this fact as I have a number of scars on my body from attempted violations of this law. Sure, you can break this law for short periods of time, but the law of gravity is always active. You can jump up, but gravity will eventually pull you down, no matter how high you jump. You can throw a ball, but gravity will pull it to earth eventually (and rather quickly for us less athletic).

You can play along with the law of gravity and have a great deal of fun. For example, there is the trampoline. The fun of a trampoline is based on the law of gravity: jump up and come down, bounce back up, come back down, bounce up again. The trampoline helps you momentarily escape gravity until you get to the top of the jump. Then gravity brings you back down. Gravity then helps to load energy, which propels you higher on the next jump. It all works great unless you miss the trampoline. Then, gravity takes over with a solid bump at the bottom.

A scar on the bottom of my chin will attest to the fact that gravity is not always my friend. While mountain biking, I involuntarily attempted to disobey the law of gravity, crashing down on my chin. I was also, at the same time, experiencing another law of physics: a body in motion will remain in motion unless acted upon by an outside force. My bike was acted upon by the outside force of a large limb (my biking buddy would tell you it was a small limb, but it was big in my memory). My front tire hit the tree limb, bringing my bike to a screeching halt, and launching me through the air. At that moment, my body was in continued motion, until gravity took over and brought me to the ground, the ground acting as a rather rude force against my motion.

You don't have to know about these laws of physics for them to act upon you. You don't have to understand the theory behind gravity for gravity to work. It will continue to act upon you, whether you like it or not. That's the nature of these laws of physics and gravity and of many other laws around us.

Guess what? There are also some Immutable Laws of Living that you may know even less about. By happenstance or good fortune, you may live within these laws. But you may also be breaking these laws without even knowing it. And you may suffer the consequences of disobeying these laws, even if you don't know these laws exist.

Over the years, I have studied these laws, mostly to see why I keep getting myself into trouble. My task has been to try to understand these laws so I could do a better job of obeying them. I'm not always successful. But the more I understand, the better I get.

The purpose of this book is to point out these Immutable Laws of Living and how to follow them. My hope is to help you understand how to live within these laws, following them as you see fit. Violating them will be at your own risk, once you know about them.

Up until now, you may have been wondering why you keep tripping yourself up. In the following pages, I hope to point out some places that are naturally getting in your way, as you unknowingly break these Immutable

Laws. Some of these laws are mindset laws (how you think about life); others are action laws (how you do things).

You will notice your mindset leads to actions, and actions can affect your mindset. Therefore, we want to approach both at the same time. Many of these laws build upon each other, so following some laws will help you follow others more easily.

One way to think of this is like being in a river. I love to paddle board. Since I don't live near the coast, my second favorite place to paddle board—a big river—is where I spend the most time. I've learned some lessons about paddling in that river. I can choose to paddle upstream, but it will take a lot more effort and lots more energy. Or, I can turn the other way and paddle downstream. Sometimes, I paddle upstream first just so I can turn around and come back downstream.

Several years ago, it was early in the season, but a warm day, so I headed off to the river with my board. At the edge of a creek, there sits a restaurant overlooking the river. I launched downstream on the creek and paddled to the river. I then turned upstream into the current of the river, with my back to the restaurant. The current was a little heavier than I had expected, the spring rains still feeding the river upstream. But, I was focused on the water flowing past me, impressed with how I was making progress. I was feeling pretty good (and imagined I was looking pretty good, as I strongly headed upriver). I paddled and paddled and paddled. My eyes were focused just ahead of my board, lost in thought, as I often am during the paddle. After about 20 minutes, I finally looked up, looked over at the bank, and realized I had not progressed more than 10 feet. As fast as I was paddling, the water was pushing me downstream. I was barely breaking even, maybe making a little progress here and there.

I became painfully aware that on this beautiful day I had lots of spectators watching me paddling in place as if I were on a treadmill. A little embarrassed, but unwilling to admit it, I calmly turned my paddleboard around and paddled back into the creek. My hope was that they believed I had done this on purpose, maybe just for a little exercise.

My point? I couldn't beat the immutable law of the power of that water. I did manage to exhaust myself. Sure, I got a little exercise. But I made no progress. Had I stood still for just a second, the river would've washed me downstream.

That's what often happens when we disobey these Immutable Laws of Living: we just don't make progress. We may not end up with a scar on our chin, but we do make life more difficult. We may be working as hard as we can, but make little progress. Life becomes frustrating. We can end up feeling defeated. And we may not have a clue about why we are not making the progress we expected. The secret is in these Immutable Laws of Living. Follow the laws, make progress. Break the laws, get stuck. We always have that choice. But you can't make that choice until you know the laws.

You will find 16 laws in the following chapters. Each chapter will introduce you to one of these laws. You will learn how we disobey these laws, and how we can obey these laws. (In other words, we will talk about how people disobey the laws with assumptions and actions.) Then, we will look at how to obey the laws in decisions and direction, so that you are working *with* them and not *against* them.

As you begin to understand each law, it will become more and more apparent in your own life and the lives of those around you. You will notice those who disobey the laws—and you will also begin to notice those who are following them. Be sure to notice the difference. Whenever someone seems to be stuck and struggling, see if you can identify which law is being broken.

Also, remember that these laws tend to build on each other. As you begin to be conscious of and work to follow one law, the other laws are easier to see and obey. Remember those laws of physics? Energy is a major component. Energy tends to flow in a set direction. Attempting to change momentum, for example, takes a great deal of energy. But if you let life do its thing and follow the laws, energy is conserved, at least to the extent it is possible.

So, let's get started with these Immutable Laws of Living.

CHAPTER 1

Life Is Not Fair

E very time "Alice" talked to me, she kept telling me stories about how she was always losing in life. In story after story, she posed herself as the victim. On this particular day, Alice told me, "Life isn't fair."

I said nothing.

She looked up at me and asked, "Aren't you going to tell me that life is somehow fair and that I will see things turn around?"

"Nope," I said, flat-toned.

She stared at me, and I stared right back. There was a long silence. She said, "You are my therapist. Aren't you supposed to make me feel better?"

I responded, "I don't think my job is to make you feel better, but to help you live a better life, build a better life, become a better person."

"What?" Alice didn't like my response.

I elaborated. I told her she kept looking for ways that life "owed" her, believing she was on the losing end of some deal. I told her she had some balance scale in her mind, where the bad stuff should be balanced with the good stuff (and perhaps even weighted toward the good side of the equation). I told her I didn't believe that was the way the world worked. I told her I didn't believe the world is meant to be fair, and I didn't believe life is meant to be fair. I also told her that wasn't really even the question.

"What IS the question, if that's not the question?" Alice asked.

I told her, "I think the question is, 'What do you do with what life gives you?'"

I could tell Alice was not satisfied with my response. I didn't expect her to be. We all have this notion, from our childhood days, where we are looking for "fair." Problem is, that is always a childhood wish.

When I was a child, we had a rule in our family between my brothers and me. Whenever there was something to share, like a cookie, one of us would divide the cookie, and the other would choose a half. It was all about equals. It was all about being fair. My parents used this approach to keep us from arguing, and probably to keep us from thinking that one parent was siding with the other sibling.

It may not surprise you that this little rule led to the most precise cutting of any cookie known on this planet. We were more accurate than a diamond cutter making the facets on a valuable diamond. Not a crumb was unevenly distributed between the two halves. Although this didn't keep us from arguing the point, even with such accuracy of division. Someone often accused the other of getting an unfair share.

We would like to think that the "fairness strategy" is true in life, too. But it isn't. Life just isn't fair—because life isn't about fairness.

I had this exact discussion with a person at a conference. His response? "Wow, you must be depressed to have such a negative view! How can you live in a world you think is unfair?"

To which I responded, "I think you are missing the point. People WANT life to be fair, but then believe it is unfair to them, in particular. Many people think THEY are not getting a fair shake in life. That the REST of the world is getting their fair share, but THEY are not. So, they believe that life SHOULD be fair, but is NOT fair to THEM, as individuals."

I continued, "I just believe there is no rule that life is fair. There is no 'fair share' to which life has entitled me. And to be crystal clear, I am not talking politics here. I am talking about the whole of life, the universe. 'Fair' is simply not a foundational, fundamental law of the universe."

How We Disobey This Law

There are three primary ways we disobey this law.

Problem #1: We tend to base this law on our own self-interest. In other words, we may quickly say to somebody who seems to be on the losing end of things, "Life isn't fair." But, we keep looking out for ourselves, wondering why life is unfair to us in particular. And that's the problem; it's based in our own self-interest. When we're looking at issues in life, we tend to focus on ourselves. That's just human nature. So the big question we all have is not whether life, in general, is unfair, but why life is unfair to *me*, in particular. We do a really good job of keeping track of all the things we want that don't come our way. We often lose track of all the things that do come our way, that drop into our lives, just out of good fortune. (And by the way, I'm never sure of the right word to use: "luck," "fortune," "blessed," or any other word. People use these words as if there is some roll of the dice or even some divine attribution.)

Sometimes, we look at how others are on the unfair "winning" end of this proposal we call life. Their life seems unfairly good to them. Maybe you know people who do bad things and still seem to end up on the winning end. Perhaps they run a dishonest business or cheat on their taxes. Perhaps they steal from work, embezzle from friends, or maybe even dip into politics. And still, they come out smelling like a rose. Their toys shine in the sun. They go on lovely vacations, always with a tan. "Life just isn't fair."

Sometimes, we secretly hold onto a belief that some "divine retribution" will come to those people. We have this sneaking hope that life will catch up with them, even things out, and make things ... fair.

But that's not how life works. That's not how the world works. That's not how the universe works. No major religion or school of philosophy has ever made the claim that life is or should be fair. In fact, the major religions and philosophies always point to the fact that that isn't even the question to ask. It would seem that much of philosophy and religion turns their attention to life *not* being fair. Because there is a bigger question.

Problem #2: It is almost always based on some material judgment. It may be about the possessions or wealth that we have or don't have. It may be about the opportunities that seem to pass us by but drop into everyone else's lap. Or maybe, it's all about the genetics. We are inundated with images of people who are wealthier, are living lives of opportunity, are "better looking," and seem to have better lives. We judge ourselves against those images.

The images bombard us through social media, through regular media, and through our imagination. More than that, we tend to judge ourselves rather harshly, even missing the fact that we have opportunities, strengths, and abilities unique to us.

But let's assume for just a moment that the world IS fair.

What would it look like? What would "fair" be? Would we all look alike, with the exact same amount of resources, living in the exact same place, with the exact family backgrounds, the same educational opportunities, and everything else being even? Would we all live the exact same amount of time, experiencing the exact same life and death?

When we start thinking about fairness from a broad perspective, it pretty much falls apart. And we arrive at the place of realizing that fairness is usually about what we want for ourselves, not what we want for everyone. As Alice once told me, "I just want my fair share."

But life isn't fair, no matter how hard we try to make it fair. Which leads to the third problem.

Problem #3: Sometimes, we use "life isn't fair" as a cop-out or avoidance. Sometimes, I watch people say, "I want what's mine!" But they don't want to struggle. They don't want to put in the effort. Sometimes, they look at somebody else's success and miss the fact that the other person may have struggled very hard to get where they are.

When we look at fairness this way, it creates a place of injustice in our minds. It gets us more focused on ourselves and less focused on what we need to do. If we are simply waiting for life to be fair, we completely disempower ourselves as we wait for life to finally "Go Fair."

This Immutable Law of Living is "Life Isn't Fair." But that's not even the issue. We can get trapped into playing this mind game, which keeps us in a child-like state, trying to divide everything cleanly. And it keeps us from living fully.

Let me just point out a few issues within this law. First, life isn't fair, but that should not be confused with injustice. This law is best applied to one's own life. It is poorly applied when aimed at someone else.

I only infrequently hear someone who is doing well, on the top of the hill, proclaim, "My life just isn't fair! I have way too much. I need to make it more fair." (Yes, there are some very wealthy people who have decided to give away their fortunes by the time—or at the time—they die. But that is a rare group, indeed. And even then, they are likely leaving a legacy of a safety net to their families.)

The nature of this world is not fairness. But there is also injustice all around us. Obeying this law is NOT the same as saying to someone suffering injustice, "Well, life just isn't fair." While I believe that life isn't fair, we work to right injustice where we can. We CAN work to make the *systems* of the world govern more fairly and justly.

That is not the same as an individual saying, "Life's not fair. I'm waiting for my fair share." (Emphasis is on "waiting.") Acting to change is great; waiting for it to change keeps you stuck.

We disobey this first law when we look at our own life while declaring "Life Isn't Fair," and then get stuck there.

How We Obey This Law

So how do we get back into obeyance of this law?

Let me suggest a few ways to make a shift:

1) Ask "How do I move from here?"

Movement, any genuine and considered movement, starts the process. When we are stuck and waiting for life to "turn fair," choosing to act is critical.

I have an acquaintance who is convinced that life is "crapping on her," leaving her with a victim mentality. Whenever things do not work out the way she would like, her first response is, "See? This just isn't fair." Ironically, in all of the other moments—the majority, I might add—where things are going just fine, she doesn't even notice.

But a single bump becomes further proof, and she stops moving. All forward progress through the day ends. She sits in a chair and says, "See?"

She only needs to choose to take action to change it all.

Years ago, I was running on a trail after a windstorm. Tree after tree was downed across the path. For a while, the trail would be clear, and I would make good progress. Then, I would come to another tree across my path. I guess I could have had a seat on the path, and decided my run was over, that "it was not meant to be," and believe that nature or God or something else was unfairly targeting my progress.

Or I could assess the situation and keep moving. At times, I went over the tree. At times, I scooted under the tree (not a pretty sight, I might add). At times, I found a way around the tree. And, at times, I had to backtrack and follow a different trail.

Every turn that led to another tree led to the question, "How do I go from here?"

When you hear yourself saying, "Life isn't fair," switch to "How do I move from here?"

2) Ask, "How do I accept the struggle as a fact, then learn, grow, and thrive?"

Acceptance starts the journey. Whatever the struggle, the obstacle is a fact. Yes, it must be faced and addressed. But it is a fact. It is there.

A major stall point is the continual struggle of accepting the struggle. We want to make it "not so." But that is rarely an effective strategy. In my years as a chaplain, I witnessed this over and over. An illness or an accident was met with a defensive "NO." We want it NOT to be there, not to have happened—to find some way to "undo it."

Almost always, that doesn't work. What has happened has happened. There may be differences in what happens from there. But rarely do we make much progress until we accept the current position and move from there.

Notice (and this is important) that I am not saying you have to accept the suggested outcome. In my years as a chaplain, I watched terminal diagnoses reverse. People who were told they could never walk went for runs; "hopeless cases" walked out the front door.

Please do not hear me say that you must accept defeat. This is about accepting the current situation—seeing it as fact—and then reorienting yourself. How can you learn, grow, and thrive, given the current situation?

3) Ask, "Can I see that life is already tipped in my favor?"

Life isn't fair. And in fact, there isn't even a scale upon which to balance it. The very fact that you and I are alive is truly amazing. The fact that we are here—me writing and you reading—is a pretty amazing thing.

Taking one step back, if you were able to visit a store or go online to purchase this book, it places you near the top of the people in the world, economically speaking. If you woke up in a bed, had a choice of clothing this morning, and had the option of getting something to eat, you are near the top of the world population in material wealth.

The fact that you are here, right now (a miracle right there), reading this book, and being mostly comfortable? You and I can truly say, "Life is not fair—and I have more than my fair share."

Life is not meant to be fair. It is agnostic about success and fairness.

And I also know, in a grander view, life is already tipped in my favor.

Human struggle is both universal and unique. All humans have disappointments, suffer losses, experience pain, and struggle to understand why this is so. And those particular struggles, disappointments, losses, and pains feel very unique when they hit you.

Whenever something tough comes along in life, it's going to be tough at ground zero. And our natural human reaction is to say, "This isn't fair."

But one step back, we see the bigger context. Life isn't about fairness, so that statement is absolutely true.

One step back: life, in and of itself, is a miracle. Scientist still can't give a good explanation of it. So until that changes, let's just accept it as a miracle.

Recently, a dear friend died. He did not live a "charmed life." His childhood was tough. His first wife was killed in a horrific car accident. He had health struggles. Yet in his last months, we shared many conversations that reiterated one powerful belief of this man, "I have been so fortunate." In his recollections, his focus was not on the tough times, but on the goodness he had encountered.

And I know a secret: he looked for the good fortune. He believed he was on the "fortunate" side of the "Life isn't fair" equation. He knew life had been tipped in his favor.

Since we all die, we can't use that as proof that "life isn't fair." So, we can either drop that equation or recognize that the question is "How do we live when life is being overly generous to us?"

4) Decide, "Life is the canvas, and I get to paint the picture." Or "Life is the marble, and I get to carve the sculpture."

Over and over through life, we realize there are some situations over which we have no control. Accidents happen, illnesses catch us, companies close, children grow up and move away, people die. We can't stop those things from happening. We rarely even have a choice of when those things happen. They just come upon us.

And yet, we get to choose the life we create—in the midst of those situations. As life goes on, we have a choice in how we craft our own lives. Yes, there are limitations and challenges. But think of it like creating art.

If you are painting, it is on a canvas. You might not like the canvas size or shape, or your options of paint colors. Still, you get to choose the scene you paint, within the confines of that canvas and those paints.

Or perhaps even more illustrative, think of life as a lump of marble. That lump sets some serious parameters on the sculpture you create. Faults and cracks limit where you can chisel. Colors and veins in the stone can alter how you shape the sculpture. Your task is to use the stone at hand, and the tools at your disposal, to create the sculpture you desire. Your design may change, based on what you discover in the stone, but you are still choosing the final sculpture you carve.

Life is not fair. It isn't in any way designed to be fair. The fact that you and I are here, right now, at this moment, is amazing. The fact that you can be learning and growing, changing your life with intention and choice, is a remarkable thing.

If we release the idea that life should be fair, we can truly live.

CHAPTER 2

Life Has Challenges

I have a memory seared into my brain from my early days as a hospital chaplain. It was a rainy Sunday night, and I was summoned to the Emergency Department. That is never a good sign. Chaplains rarely get called to the Emergency Department to celebrate a happy outcome.

The hospital had a couple of family rooms just off the waiting room. In moments of tragedy, or potential tragedy, families were gathered into those rooms so they could process information and be together in difficult times.

Earlier that night, a young man failed to stop for a red light, plowing through the intersection and into a car proceeding through on a green light. Another young man was in the other car. Two young men, out on a rainy evening. Their lives intersected in that accident.

And each family was in one of the rooms.

The young man who failed to stop had a few stitches on his forehead and bruising from the seatbelt and airbag. But he would go home that night.

The other young man had died in the ER from massive internal trauma.

It was a tragic accident, and these two families were now in the midst of struggling with what had happened. My role was to be with both families as they processed their emotions and thoughts.

Both families struggled with "Why?" Why did the accident happen? Why was their loved one spared or killed? Why?

We all struggle with these tough questions whenever something unexpected happens in life. We don't ask when things are proceeding along fine, everything going as we expect. We ask when our expectations are uprooted.

In one room, the family had their own answer to "Why?" They were giving God credit for saving their family member.

In the other room, the family also had their own answer to "Why?" They were blaming God for taking their family member from them.

After a bit, a family member turned to me and asked, "Why did God do this?" I suggested that laws of physics had caused this. Momentum and inertia affected the impact. Two objects can't occupy the same space. Power was transferred from the one car to the other. I didn't give a long explanation of physics but simply said that I believed it was not God who *caused* the accident. That was a failure of action by a person. The laws of physics created the outcome.

There is a base reality to life: Challenges happen.

Why do we ask why? For two reasons. First, we would love to somehow have a reason for why things happen. Second, we would love to find a way to have them not happen. In other words, "Why did this happen?" is often another way of asking, "Is there a way for this to NOT happen?"

We humans love to try to find a way to turn reality away from what it is, toward a reality we would rather have.

But here is the Immutable Law of Living: Life Has Challenges.

Every single life, every single person, faces a world of challenges. If we look around, this is pretty evident. Life is a rough-and-tumble existence. Our ancestors knew this. Threats lurked behind every tree or rock. Illnesses had no treatment. Lack of resources, including food and water, could happen at any time. There was no warning for weather. Life had challenges. Every day.

In our modern world, we like to think we can control the world around us. We try our best to make our environment safe, protect our loved ones, and avoid bad things from happening.

Yet they still do.

We just pretend they *shouldn't*. So when there is a challenge, we believe it to be an aberration. Challenges, though, are a part of life.

But they don't just happen TO us. We help in causing some of them. Then, we rail against them.

Another late night in the hospital as a chaplain, another moment seared into my mind. I was summoned to the Oncology ward of the hospital. People there were being treated for cancer, either surgically, chemotherapeutically, or both. I was called in to see "Fred."

As I knocked and opened the door, I could see the glow and smell the smoke of a cigarette. This happened in the days when they still allowed patients to smoke in the room. All while he was breathing pure oxygen through his nose. I was smart enough to recognize the senselessness of letting a patient smoke, much less with the explosive potential of pure oxygen. But those were the rules of the day.

I introduced myself and asked if I could sit down. Fred consented, ever staring at the ceiling, puffing on his cigarette. I sat and asked, "Fred, they told me you wanted a chaplain. How can I help?"

Without breaking his stare, Fred said, "Chaplain, I have lung cancer. They said they can't do much for me. I'm going to die."

"I am sorry to hear that Fred. It must be hard to process all that so quickly." I tried to respond empathetically.

He continued, "Chaplain, my question is, why did God do this to me? Why did God give me cancer?"

As a chaplain, you get that question quite often.

"Fred, before I answer, could I ask you a question?" I stalled.

"Sure."

"Fred, how long have you been smoking?" I sheepishly asked.

He told me he started smoking when he was 13. Now, 45 years later, he smoked over two packs a day. Every day.

"Fred, do you think that maybe the smoking had something to do with this?" I gingerly asked.

It was a long silence. Then Fred said, "I suppose it might." We sat quietly as Fred processed a tough thought: he might have created his own challenge. I say "might have," knowing that science is on my side. But I also know that there are many other people with the exact same habit who will escape cancer.

Life has challenges for everyone. Some are tied to our own actions. We do things that place ourselves at risk. And, corporately, we have done things that place all of us at risk. We create our own risks in the world around us. In other words, as humans, many of those challenges are self-created.

Some challenges just happen. We are in the wrong place at the wrong time. Forces of nature strike. Gravity catches up with us. We are infected by microorganisms that surround us. As that bumper sticker says it, "Sh*! Happens."

And then there are those combinations. The intersection between our actions and bad stuff happening. We place ourselves into dangerous situations. We don't take precautions when we know we should. We take chances in risky situations.

In other words, challenges happen of our own doing, from outside forces, and from a combination. Stuff happens in life.

Over the years, I have had a number of discussions with highly successful people. To the person, they all have a story of failure. Many built and lost companies repeatedly. Most suffered economic ruin at some point, only to rebuild and find success.

Every one of them told me the same thing: their current success came from skills learned in those failures. And not all of the failures were their fault. One person was a developer who started a project six months before the housing collapse. The project made sense when he started. But when the market collapsed, it took his company with it. The project sat for years, incomplete. And he rebuilt, learning his lessons from the market collapse—even though he had nothing to do with creating that collapse.

Whether these successful people made mistakes or just happened to be faced with unforeseen circumstances, every single one told the same story, "My success today is a direct result of the lessons I learned in the struggles."

Life has challenges. That's the law.

Quick question: If you wanted to build some muscle, what would you do? Let's say you want to show off some nice biceps next summer, or you want to be in better shape. What would you do?

I can tell you what I did when I made that decision: I picked up heavy stuff. I lifted weights. And I would lift a weight until I couldn't. I lifted until, as the trainer would say, "muscle failure." In other words, I challenged the muscle—until it was exhausted. Then, I would come back and challenge it again.

We all have a "challenge muscle." This is a psychological muscle that is strengthened when we take on life's challenges. But many times, we let this muscle atrophy. Sometimes, people decide to avoid problems, run from them, and admit defeat. When something is challenging, some will proclaim, "I can't do it," or "It can't be done," and walk away.

Admittedly, some challenges simply cannot be overcome. Sometimes, a challenge ends a possibility. When the housing market crashed, no amount of creative accounting or special financing was going to save the developer's company. He was under water and had to close it down.

But even those challenges have points of growth. The developer closed his company, paid off his contractors and vendors (adding hugely to his own debt), and looked for another opportunity. He could have given up, decided the world was just unfair, and accepted defeat.

Instead, he rebuilt. He learned the lessons he could, retooled, looked for opportunity, and moved on. The challenge gave him new skills and capacities.

Challenges can be growth points. They can point us toward a new future—but only when we struggle through.

If you have children, we probably have some very similar memories. During those first few years, you watch a child hit a point of growth where the child wants more capacity than their little body allows. So, the child grows discontent and works toward a new skill.

I remember my two children in their attempts to walk. First, they would pull up on furniture, only to plop back down on diapered bottoms. Then they would try again. Once up, there was maybe one step before another plop to the ground. But soon, those children are cruising around, holding on to objects for stability and safety. Then comes the release—and a plop back to the ground. But eventually, that child is walking (and a parent's life is forever changed to chasing!).

At no point have I ever seen a child plop to the ground and proclaim, "Well, I guess I am just not meant to walk. Guess I'll just stay here."

Nope. They pull back up and try again. At that point in life, the challenge muscle is pretty strong. And it is strengthened by every next challenge.

There comes a time when many of us forget about this muscle. We might start with that little belief, "Life should be fair," and then add one more piece: "There shouldn't be any challenges." In other words, we come to secretly believe that if we are struggling, something is wrong. Somewhere, we come to believe that life should NOT be a challenge—and if it is, it indicates that there is something unfair and wrong going on.

How We Disobey This Law

This law is a mindset law. In other words, we disobey this law by what we believe. Our belief is what leads to action (or in this case, inaction).

1) We believe that difficulties in life indicate something is wrong with our life. When it gets tough, we decide, "Life shouldn't be this way." For example, in my work with married couples, I hear, "If our relationship was meant to be, it wouldn't be a struggle. It should just work."

Where else do we apply that in life? "If I was supposed to be in shape, it would just happen. I wouldn't have to exercise." "If I was meant to survive this illness, it would just happen. No need to get treatment." "If I was meant to be in that profession, I would just have that job. No need for getting that education."

The fact is, we don't apply that mindset to many areas of our lives. But in relationships, personal development and growth, and often around money—there, we assume that difficult times mean something is wrong.

2) We view life from failure, not challenge. Things get tough, people walk away. But in my conversations with those highly successful people? The difficult times came just before the breakthrough. The roadblocks provided the last necessary information to get to the other side.

When Thomas Edison was looking for the perfect filament, a reporter asked how it felt to have failed so many times. Edison is reported to have replied, "Failed? I now know 10,000 things that won't work."

3) When we hit difficulties, we assign meaning to it: "God doesn't love me," "The world is out to do me in," "I must not be a good person," "I'm too (foolish/stupid/insignificant/etc.) to do this." In other words, we let the struggle takes us back to "Life isn't fair."

How We Obey This Law

There is one advantage to a law of mindset: you can always choose to change your mindset. As soon as you see the limitations, you can always choose a more expansive way of thinking. That shifts you into obeying the law. But you do need to know the mindset and see the shift that is possible.

Here are some shifts to make:

1) Be clear that life is not one long, smooth, progression line upward. The line has fits and starts, fails, struggles, successes, rest points, and repetition. And the line is more of a curling, whirling line across the page of life. When things are upward, there will be a struggle. When things are downward, there will be a shift. "I'm ruined" is rarely the final word, and "I finally made it to the top" is often followed by another challenge.

2) See challenges as data points. Any roadblock can be seen as either failure or data point. Failure is the point when you are no longer willing to move forward. It is when you give up. Choose to see those same instances as data points. Thomas Edison was collecting data points. A data point is information, feedback. It tells you what won't work. It demonstrates there may need to be an alternate route. Data points are just feedback for life. Decide to see those difficult moments as data points.

3) Take on challenges as learning opportunities. In her excellent book, *Mindset*, Carol Dweck notes the difference between a "growth mindset" and a "fixed mindset." In a growth mindset, you see yourself as constantly growing and developing. In a fixed mindset, you see a trait or skill as inborn and set. For example, a child may be seen as "a natural athlete." But such a mindset keeps you limited. If you are a "natural," then you shouldn't need to practice or try.

A growth mindset is when you take on challenges as opportunities for growth. When Dweck was studying young children, the children were asked to put together puzzles of varying difficulty. Some pouted and gave up when the puzzle was a struggle. But others rolled up their sleeves, rubbed their hands together, and proclaimed, "I love a good challenge."

Decide to see the challenges as opportunities to grow and develop new skills. Challenges are the fuel of growth. If we don't take on challenges, we don't grow. Without growth, we are stagnant. Whatever skills you have can be further refined and developed. But only when challenges are seen as opportunities, not roadblocks.

4) Ask yourself, "Given this, what now?"

When a challenge hits, you can always ask that question. No matter how big the challenge. A career setback, a financial crisis, an illness, a relationship crisis—you can respond to any challenge with "Given this, what now?"

Notice, it does not pretend that nothing happened. The question starts with clarity on exactly what did happen. But the next part frees you to think of "next" when the crisis can have you in "stuck."

Over the millennia, people have had life-altering crises that led to a whole new life. Many times, that life had more depth, meaning, and purpose than the prior life. New companies, relationships, occupations, organizations, and opportunities have been built on challenges that may have seemed more like failures. But they only unfold when someone ponders, "Given this, what now?"

I believe humans are designed to find meaning in events, follow purpose in their lives, and make an impact in the world. Life challenges are often the starting point for discovering meaning and purpose, and for making an impact in the world

And those challenges remind us that we are connected to other people and to the rest of the universe. Because we all have challenges.

The real struggle? Letting go of the prior life—life "BC" (before challenge). Many times, we are attached to the world we know and want to go back to it. But that world no longer exists after a major challenge. That prior existence is gone. What replaces it, though, may be a bigger world. There will always be some feelings of grief and loss when those challenges hit. Expect to be caught in the grief. But decide the grief does not prevent moving forward and discovering new possibilities. Grief is processing what was, but it is a bridge to what now is.

I have a soft spot for sea turtles. They seem so calm, so clumsy. And yet, they are graceful in their element. I've been approached by more than a few on my diving excursions.

On a beach where we vacation, every spring the mama turtles return and lay a nest of eggs way up in the dunes, safe from the tides. Later in the summer, these eggs hatch in what they call a "boil," with potentially over a hundred little turtles clamoring over each other to make a trek to the ocean, their new home.

That struggle to the sea is wrought with danger. First, it is a long slog over uneven sand. Second, they are following the light of the moon (nests usually boil when the sand cools at night), and sometimes the moon is hidden or other lights cause confusion. Third, they are tasty treats for other beach dwellers; birds, raccoons, foxes, and feral cats are all waiting for a moving buffet line. And then, after they make it to the water, they need to be fast. Ocean dwellers are also waiting for a meal delivery.

We can't do much to protect them in the ocean. But many towns along the beach have a "turtle brigade" that monitors the nests. When it is time for a hatch, they await the turtles and escort them down to the waves. Notice, I said "escort" and not "carry." Visitors are given very strict instructions on multiple occasions to NOT handle those baby turtles.

One night, my family and I were hoping to see a boil. We were posted near the nest, kept at a safe distance by the turtle brigade volunteers. I was chatting with one volunteer about this very precarious trip to the sea. Only about one in a thousand turtles will make it to adulthood. So, getting as many of them into the ocean as possible is paramount to species survival. This volunteer told me of all the dangers and struggles to get there.

I asked, "Given the dangers to just get to the water, why not just pick them up and carry them down? Why not give them a head start? Skip the first danger? Why make them crawl the gauntlet?"

She smiled and told me, "We have discovered that in the struggle to get to the water's edge, the turtles are activating and building the muscles in the legs. As they crawl, the struggle over the sand activates the muscles and builds them up. If we just carried them down, they would not be able to swim when they hit the water. They would drown. And if they could swim enough to stay up, they would not be able to swim efficiently enough to avoid being a snack along the way."

The struggle on the way to the ocean? It gave them the strength to take on the challenge of the ocean. One struggle is preparing them for the next struggle. The first struggle is necessary for the next, bigger struggle.

Life does not let us go back. But it does allow us to move forward. Challenges build the muscle for the climb (or the next swim).

Life is full of challenges. They prepare us for the next stage in life. The challenges we face as children prepare us for the challenges of adolescence. The adolescent challenges prepare us for young adulthood. And those challenges? They prepare us to live our purpose, to make an impact in the world. We can make that impact at any time. But often, it is rooted in the challenges we have overcome. Muscles capable of impact are built in the challenges.

CHAPTER 3

Life Isn't About Happiness

In the United States' Declaration of Independence, our Founding Fathers wrote that we, as a people, have a right to "life, liberty, and the pursuit of happiness." It says it right there. We have a "right to happiness."

Right?

Over the years, many unhappy people have given me this reason for why they believe they deserve to be happy—they have a "right" to be happy. And yet, they are miserable.

First, the idea of "happiness," as stated in the Declaration, is not quite the same as our idea of happiness these days. In our modern culture, that "pursuit of happiness" has more in common with hedonism, the pursuit of what feels good. Often, that hedonism sends people into "short-term feel-goods." Very rarely does that pursuit lead to long-term satisfaction or joy. It has a much more if-it-feels-good-do-it vibe—which often has consequences.

Any number of these "feel-good" pursuits can lead to long-term problems. They tend to be excesses that take a toll on our physical health and on our relationships.

But to return to that Declaration, Thomas Jefferson was penning a phrase based on a history of philosophy. He was pulling from the Greek idea of "Eudaimonia." This term is more related to virtue and excellence. The philosopher, Aristotle, stated the happy person lives well and does well. It was tied to living virtues. In his book, *Nicomachean Ethics*, Aristotle wrote, "…the function of man is to live a certain kind of life, and this activity implies a rational principle, and the function of a good person is the good and noble performance of these, and if any action is well performed it is performed in accord with the appropriate excellence: if this is the case, then happiness turns out to be an activity of the soul in accordance with virtue."

Jefferson, a fan of Aristotle, believed that happiness is bound up with the civic virtues of courage, moderation, and justice.

Humans, I believe, are not here just to find happiness (in our current vernacular). Life isn't about happiness.

Just to clarify, I am not suggesting you need to be miserable and unhappy. Just because life is not about happiness does not mean life is about unhappiness. Life is much more agnostic about happiness. It just isn't about that. There is nothing wrong with being happy. But happiness is more a side effect than anything pursued. And to further clarify, I am not saying you need to just "suck it up" and accept whatever and wherever you are.

That said, I have noticed a very powerful and common belief among clients of mine: if you aren't happy, you should get away from what is making you unhappy. This belief comes from a person believing they *should* be happy. So, they leave marriages and careers, all in the "pursuit of happiness," only to discover the new person or new job didn't make a long-term difference. They forgot that wherever they went, they were taking themselves along for the ride. The pursuit of happiness led to further unhappiness.

When I met "Bill," he was on his third marriage and sixth career. In both his current marriage and his current career, he was miserable. Bill told me about his slog through the day, every day, waiting for the weekend. On the weekend, he played golf for hours or rode his bike for hours. Bill drank too much, spent too much, and was still miserable. All by the age of 48.

Bill was in my office because it was slowly dawning on him that perhaps the problem was not the women he married or the work he did. Perhaps it was something else. Bill was beginning to think that perhaps this had something to do with him. He was admittedly still unsure.

As we spoke, I noted to Bill that he kept telling me about things that "made" him happy or unhappy. I asked him another question: "What, Bill, is important to you?" Bill was a bit perplexed. It seemed that question didn't occur to him.

Bill switched back to his model, "I married my first wife because she made me happy. We were so in love. I just felt good when she was around. But she started nagging. She started demanding things. I wasn't happy. I realized she wasn't going to be able to make me happy, so I left."

That same story marked Bill's second marriage and was now invading his third. That same story came out about work, too. He started at a bank. That made him unhappy, so he left to be a mortgage broker. That was a miserable experience, so he started his own company. THAT certainly made him miserable! So, he became a mid-level manager for a company. His boss? Made him miserable. His staff? They were miserable. So, he left and returned to a bank job. Still miserable there, so he became a real estate agent. There he was successful—and miserable.

Throughout the story, there was one central theme: Bill believed that someone should make him happy. Bill believed that some job should make him happy. Bill believed that life was about being happy.

He told me, "All I want is to be happy. That's what I want."

"Bill," I suggested, "perhaps you are chasing the wrong thing. Life isn't meant to make you happy."

As humans often do, Bill concluded that if it was not one thing, it must be the opposite. "So," he huffed, "I should just be unhappy and miserable? Life isn't worth much if I'm miserable."

I continued, "Bill, what if life just isn't about being happy or unhappy? What if life is not about happiness? What if your comfort or discomfort isn't really built into the fabric of life? Is it possible that life is about something else?"

Objectively, I think we can all see this. Yes, humans have chased happiness for quite some time. But I doubt our ancient ancestors pondered much about "Is my life happy? Am I getting my fair share of happiness?" It just wasn't in the equation. Survival and safety ranked a bit higher. Perhaps there has been a certain progression to where we are:

"I want to feel safe."

"I want to feel comfortable."

"I want to feel happy."

"I deserve to be happy."

And on that last progression, we shift from *desire* to *right*. If we are unhappy, then something is unfair (see the last Immutable Law) or wrong. But notice that we are in the scope of feelings. Feeling safe is partly a by-product of creating a safe environment (although it is entirely possible to *be* safe and not *feel* safe, or to *feel* safe and not *be* safe). The same is true with comfort.

Here is the problem with these levels: they are at least partly subjective. One person's level of safety and comfort is another person's level of fear and discomfort. And the same is true with happiness. What makes one person happy may mean nothing to another. It is an entirely subjective experience.

Life isn't about happiness. But I also do not think that this means life is about nothing.

About this time, that little thought starts sneaking in for some people. Bill said it best, "If life is not about being happy, then what IS it about? Is life just about me stumbling through, miserable and unhappy, waiting to die?" That's the sneaky little thought.

Wow. No.

When I look around, I notice that there is something of an innate purpose or design to things. A tree does what a tree does. If it is a fruit tree, it grows up and produces fruit. Or it grows to produce shade. Its purpose is built into the design. The same with animals. Animals follow a design built into them. You can even say the same about microorganisms. As far as we can tell, a bacterium is not angry, setting out to make you sick (and in fact, your body is filled with bacteria and other microorganisms that help you to stay healthy). Bacteria *can* make you sick. But it is just doing its thing, its design.

What, then, is built into the human design? Humans have that unique capacity to think and ponder. I believe that humans have, as part of our design, the capacity for meaning, purpose, and impact. I believe life is much more about finding your purpose, discovering deep meaning, and making an impact in the world around you. It's in your design.

How that design forms for you? *That* is your unique impact, your unique place of meaning and purpose. I just know that it is already within you, emerging or waiting to emerge.

How We Disobey This Law

Many of us wholeheartedly believe, whether we are or not, that we *should* be happy. We believe this is what life is about. So, we constantly chase after it, with happiness being elusive and just out of reach. We chase harder and harder, not noticing that just as we catch up to happiness, it moves just a little further away.

Our solution is to chase harder. In the process, we often cause harm to ourselves (and others). We indulge in too many things that we believe will make us happy. We also tend to avoid the areas we believe might *not* make us happy. People try to use outside things to bring in happiness. We eat foods that are too rich, take substances that might alter our mood, and chase experiences that we believe will bring happiness. At the same time, we avoid the drudgery of activities we believe will not bring happiness (even ones necessary to progress healthily through life).

In the process, we damage ourselves, our families, our community, and our world.

So, the first way we disobey this law: We constantly pursue happiness with what we think will make us happy (though it rarely moves the "happy" needle for very long).

And because we believe we should be happy, when we are not, we come to believe that something is innately wrong in the world. Either something is wrong with me or with the world around me if I am not happy. Which leads to more internal pressure to find happiness, along with a now-built-in belief that something *must* be wrong if we are not happy. This is the second way we disobey this law.

Which also leads to a third violation: creating a reason why one is not happy:

1. Life isn't fair (see Law #1).
2. Something is wrong with you.
3. God hates you/is punishing you. (Your concept of God is irrelevant here; you just have a sneaky suspicion that God—however you envision God—is against you.)

How We Obey This Law

As we have already discussed, life has built-in challenges. They come upon us, regardless of who we are and what we do. Life just has challenges. When a challenge hits, if you have a belief that "life is about happiness," you might default to seeing it not as a challenge, but as unhappiness. So, if life is supposed to be happy, side-step the challenge. Avoid it, rail against it, and see it as unfair.

Or, see that life is not fair (as we have discussed—and remember, you and I are on the winning end of it), nor is it about happiness. It IS about growth. The number one way to start obeying this law? See challenges as an opportunity for growth. See the challenge as having the potential to grow and strengthen you, so that you live out your life design.

The next step in obeying this law is to focus on living out your human design:

1. **Meaning**
2. **Purpose**
3. **Impact**

The *Meaning/Purpose/Impact Triad* is our deepest need. We have a need to make sense of the world—to find meaning. We have a need to feel a direction—a purpose. And we have a need to make a difference—have impact. Whenever we feel we can't make a difference, an impact in the world (because our actions are limited, or our role is limited), we still want some sense of purpose. If we don't feel we can move with purpose (because of limitations upon us), we still want to make sense of life—find meaning. We are at our optimal, though, when we find meaning, move with purpose, and make an impact.

People find themselves in a crisis when they cannot find meaning, find their purpose, and make a difference. And you will notice that none of these is explicitly about finding happiness. Ironically, deep life satisfaction and joy are the outcomes of a meaningful, purposeful, impactful life.

Think back for a moment on a time when you had a sense of purpose. A time when things just made sense. A time when you could see you made a difference for others. Perhaps it was a volunteer situation. Or maybe it was at work. Or it could be as a parent or grandparent. Did you feel deep satisfaction? Did you, perhaps even in the midst of difficult circumstances, find joy and bliss?

"Happiness" begins to feel a bit light and shallow when compared to this deeper sense of joy and bliss. And it can come in the direst of circumstances. I have spoken with people who have devoted their lives to the most destitute or in the midst of tragic circumstances who still report this deeper level of life satisfaction. They may struggle to label it bliss, given their surroundings. But they certainly describe a deep level of life satisfaction.

Many such people have told me about an internal shift that happened. They went from feeling scarcity to feeling gratitude. They shifted from feeling like they "didn't have enough" to feeling like their "life was overflowing." Same circumstances, different perspective. They found gratitude. This is a shift we can choose at any time.

Shift thinking to gratitude. We will discuss this more in a later chapter. But for now, understand that humans are not good at shifting their thinking to "being happy." Happiness stays elusive, no matter how much you try to convince yourself to "just be happy." Our brain really has two phases: threat/fear and love/appreciation. Given some pretty deep wiring, we often default to threat/fear (which does keep happiness at a good distance). But we don't have to live by default. Humans also have the capacity of *choosing* love/gratitude. By focusing on the things over which you are grateful, you make a shift to being grateful. Which causes a shift in your brain phase. When focused on gratitude, you are less dominated by threat/fear.

Shift from a search for happiness to a search for meaning/purpose/impact. In the process, your mind will shift away from scarcity toward gratitude. Your mind will shift from "the world isn't fair" to a recognition that fairness isn't even the issue. When we shift to a place of giving, we escape the need for getting. We end up making a difference.

CHAPTER 4

Thoughts Are Just Thoughts

W e humans do have that gift/curse of thinking. But, we tend to miss the most important aspect of our thinking: it is just thoughts. Your mind is designed to create thoughts. That's just what it does. Nothing wrong with that—until we forget they are just thoughts.

If I were to ask you what you did three Mondays ago, you might struggle to recall the exact day. But if you keep a decent calendar and I asked you to look at it, you would likely be able to start with one piece of your schedule, say a meeting, and reconstruct much of the day.

If it was a vivid event—a holiday, an accident, an "out of the ordinary" day—you would likely be able to tell me all about it. Our memories (which are just *thoughts* about past events, pulled into the current moment) let us remember the event and re-live it. You might even notice that recalling those vivid events creates an emotional response in your body. (And you might also note that the thoughts of those events, your memories, are imperfect and flawed. In reality, you are *thinking* about those events, not recalling the actual events.)

And something might happen right now, yet you are not experiencing that specific event as much as you are thinking about that event. Yesterday, I received a call from a scammer. He wanted me to believe my computer had "issues." I knew it from the moment he called. But I decided to play along. I was taking a work break, and I reasoned that if I wasted his time, he had less time to go scam someone else. So, I played along—and pretended to be fairly clueless, so as to waste even more time.

We got to the point when he wanted me to download a remote control and let him start "fixing" my computer. That was where I was unwilling to go. All along, I had been calm, until I expressed to him that I knew he was scamming, that he had no right to take advantage of people, and that his conscience should be making him feel bad. When I expressed that, my anger spiked! My thoughts, when expressed, caused me to get very angry. That call ended abruptly. He hung up.

After a few minutes, I calmed down. I moved on and did some other things, shifting myself away from those thoughts.

When my wife came home, I told her about it, recalling the events. And I became angry again! The event had happened over an hour before. I was just telling her the story—and was re-experiencing my emotions tied to the thoughts.

The power of thoughts.

If I were to ask you to make yourself angry (sad, happy, or even anxious), what would you do? If you are like all of the people I have ever asked to do this same thing in a workshop, you would think about something that made you angry (sad, happy, or anxious). You would re-experience the emotions of the event as you recalled (thought about) the event.

(I stopped using this experiment at a workshop for one simple reason: generally, I had turned a room full of jovial people who were feeling good into a room full of angry people, partly angry at me for getting them into this state! But you are not with me ... so I hope you aren't too upset right now.)

Thoughts are just what our mind does. Our mind spins thought after thought throughout the day. And those thoughts leave us in different emotional states. Not because of the event, but because of the thoughts we think about that event.

There is the event, and there are the thoughts about that event. They are not the same thing. Sometimes, we forget this, as they seem to be happening simultaneously; we think the thoughts are the event. This is true about big events and mundane events.

As I write this, it is early morning. If I look out my window, I could even claim it to be night. Still dark. It is my habit and ritual to get up and write before the day starts. Many days, this is my only opportunity to write and not be distracted.

So objectively, I have made a decision to get up early and write. Objectively, I am sitting in my kitchen and writing. Subjectively, some mornings I am ready to get up and write. I am happy and ready to get to it. Other mornings, I have to have a discussion with myself to not hit the snooze (at least more than once), to get out of a warm bed and head to my computer. Same event each morning, yet very different thoughts about that event, including my emotional state which emerges from the thoughts (not the event—it is the same every day).

Your mind thinks. That's what a mind does. The problem is not in your thinking, but in your *forgetting* that you are thinking. I have nothing against thinking. I tend to do a good bit of it every day. The question is how closely we live with our thoughts, believing that thoughts are reality. If we live too closely to thoughts, we let our thoughts rule our lives, to the point of being held prisoner by them.

Let's imagine you are driving to work, perhaps headed to a downtown office. On the way, you've been thinking about your day, listening to the news and thinking about the stories you hear, and maybe even thinking back to that "discussion" you had on the way out the door with your spouse or child. It is probably safe to say that you are living more in your thoughts than in the moment.

As you approach a light and stop, you notice a person staring at you intently. "Huh," you think. "I wonder what that was about." Objective reality: you stopped at a light, and there was a person on the corner, seemingly looking in your direction.

The light turns green, and you proceed through the intersection. As you do, your thoughts turn to that person. "Did I pull up too close to him? Was it someone I know? Did I almost hit him? Did I make some mistake in my driving?" As you are thinking, you are becoming more agitated and upset. You start feeling bad about yourself and even your driving. "I should have paid more attention," you tell yourself. And in the process, you miss your turn and continue three more blocks, lost in your thoughts—and feeling pretty bad about yourself.

A more objective observation might have helped you notice a white cane with a red tip in the hands of the stranger. His "intent staring" was really him being intentionally attentive, so he could safely cross a busy road. If you had noted that, your likely emotional response would have been empathetic and caring. Instead, thanks to your thoughts, you are a bit peeved at yourself and this person.

Thoughts.

Our thoughts lead to great things—and to horrible things. The same thought process can imagine and build a great, tall skyscraper or plot the destruction of that same building. Both begin in thought. Thoughts lead to emotions. Emotions lead to action. When we forget we are thinking, our emotions and actions often come from a "thought reality," which is not nearly as objective as we like to pretend. Thanks to thoughts, we really do not see things as they are. We see things as we think them to be.

Let me be clear, the human capacity for thought is truly amazing. Thoughts can cause amazing amounts of human suffering, often regardless of external conditions and objective realities. I have a dear friend who has an objectively outstanding life. Living in a nice house in a nice neighborhood—bills always paid, food always available, and able to take trips around the world—she feels unhappy. Her thoughts are often focused on other people being angry with her and not liking her. She always thinks she is on the losing end of situations. And because of those thoughts, she misses out on her opportunities and rich life. Instead, she is often miserable. More than that, since she believes people are against her and angry with her, she often responds defensively. Not surprisingly, this often creates tense situations with others—leading them to be angry with her. It creates a self-fulfilling reality.

For a moment, let's think of thoughts not as "good" or "bad," but as "helpful" or "not helpful." Reality tends to be fairly neutral. We can *think* about reality as good or bad. These thoughts might be helpful or not helpful. Does it help us live a life of meaning and purpose, or does it keep us stuck, fearful, and angry? If a thought is helpful, great! It is still a thought, but it is a helpful thought. If a thought is not helpful, it is important to note the thought is really just a thought. Since we create thoughts, we can also decide how tightly we hold to a thought. If we can create a thought, it is also possible to drop a thought.

Imagine a line:

Thought Reality

Thought Recognition

This is the spectrum of our Thought Awareness. How aware are we, at any point in time, that a thought is just a thought, versus a belief that a thought is reality? At one end is "Thought Reality"—a thought arises, and we believe it to be true. At the other end is "Thought Recognition"—we recognize a thought is just a thought. In between, we find the gradient of our thinking lives, where we more or less recognize a thought as a thought and more or less believe a thought to be reality. We mostly live in a span in the middle.

At the one end, where every thought is a reality, we find mental illness. What an unhappy place to exist! Any thought or notion that pops into the mind is believed as real. Generally, the very furthest point on that end is represented by severe schizophrenia. When I was in training, I consulted in the emergency room, dealing with patients experiencing severe mental illness. It was amazing to see how strongly a person held to beliefs and thoughts as they emerged. Because of the thoughts, they were living in an alternate world.

At the other end, where thoughts are recognized as thoughts, we find fewer people than at the first end. This would be a person that, no matter what was happening, had an awareness of the thinking process going on. As they are thinking, they are fully aware of the thinking, not confusing the thoughts with reality.

To be clear, I am not saying there is no "real world." There are those who believe that we actually create ALL of reality in our thoughts. This is not about creating reality, as much as molding our own reality based on the thoughts we are having about the objective world.

Just because I have a thought doesn't make it real. But reality, as I experience it, is shaped by my thoughts—at least to the degree that I am not aware of my thinking. When I recognize I am thinking, it helps me to shift back to a *more* objective experience.

Let's say things are not going well in my business. Objectively, sales are down, and staffing is not effective. We can see the objective measurement about that. Let's say that this triggers a cascade of thoughts: "This business is doomed," "I never should have gotten into this," "I can't handle this," "I'm not good at anything," "I am a failure." Notice the cascade? Have you ever had a similar thought cascade? Down and down it goes, all taking you deeper and deeper into an emotionally negative response.

Let's look again at that same situation: Sales are down and staffing isn't effective. I could see that fact objectively and begin to put together a plan on turning things around. I might hire new staff, find a consultant, create a marketing campaign, look at trimming costs, or any number of other interventions. Notice, this path also includes thoughts. But likely, more helpful thoughts.

What if, in the first scenario, I am able to step back and say, "Wow, look at my thoughts. I'm having a negative thought cascade. I need to let that go." And, recognizing that this cascade is not reality, I let the thoughts drop. I no longer prop them up, "entertain" them, dwell on them, and believe them.

The difference is not whether thinking happens, but whether I believe the thoughts or recognize them as simply thoughts.

Place yourself on the *Thought Awareness Spectrum*. Where do you fall? It is likely a range. On days when you are rested, and your mood is better, you likely notice more thoughts for what they are. But when you are tired, and your mood is lower, you probably move further down the line, toward "Thought Is Reality." I say this because it is absolutely true for me.

How can you shift a little further toward Thought Recognition? This is really a matter of awareness of the nature of thoughts. As soon as you recognize you are thinking, you shift toward the right of the scale. And you likely notice that your emotional response is more positive.

You don't have to stop thinking. You just have to realize you are thinking. That is a much easier order. Since your mind is designed to think, it is very difficult to turn it off. But the less you buy into your thoughts as reality, the better you get at moderating your thinking.

How We Disobey This Law

When we believe our thoughts are real, we disobey this Immutable Law: A thought is just a thought. In reality, most of us disobey this law multiple times per day. In fact, if you are struggling with this very idea of your thoughts just being thoughts, you likely disobey this law quite frequently. And we all are more likely to disobey this law when we are tired, don't feel well, or are overwhelmed (often less by reality and more by our thoughts, I might add).

For example, let's say I get an angry letter from someone who disagrees with something I have said or written. (It is not an infrequent occurrence.) If I am tired, I can spend energy letting it reflect upon my intellect, skills, decency as a human—and descend down to unhelpful thoughts and emotions. If I am rested and feeling better, I can recognize that not everyone will agree with me. I can let that letter just be that person's response—not a reflection on me. To be clear, I read those same letters for feedback. Perhaps I could explain things better, or perhaps I overstated something. But maybe this is just the other person's response, and I can leave it at that.

When I believe the thought in my head is reality, I am violating this law—and creating an unhelpful emotional response.

The second way we disobey this law is a direct follow-up to the first: IF I believe my thoughts are real, I will also believe my thoughts are accurate. I will not see them as my subjective beliefs, but as an objective reality, and I will act accordingly.

In other words, I will believe myself to be right and others (with differing views) to be wrong. I will not view it as "just seeing things from another perspective," but objectively wrong. Our beliefs about the world are partly thoughts passed on to us and partly our own thoughts. Again, this does not negate an objective reality. As we will talk about in the next Immutable Law, our thoughts are partly original creation and partly based on beliefs (thoughts) we have absorbed through others around us, the culture in which we find ourselves, and other factors.

While there is an objective reality, our views on that reality are very subjective.

(This is a dangerous rabbit hole, but let's explore it for a second. If you were here with me as I write this, you would likely agree that there is a table upon which my laptop is sitting. We would objectively agree to it. Quantum physicists might argue that the table is more empty space than solid—so there is some subjectivity even in our objective reality. Nonetheless, we would probably agree there is a table right here. Let's just call that the objective reality. I might think, "Isn't it nice that this table is here to hold my laptop and give me a workspace?" You might think, "Why would someone put this table here, in my way? I need this space! How dare someone place it here!" The same "objective reality." But very different subjective responses to that reality. And both responses are just thoughts.)

How We Obey This Law

When we would rather stop fighting this law, we can obey it pretty easily by recognizing that:

1. **We are thinking**

2. They are just thoughts

This was a game-changer in my own life. Before realizing this, I would wrestle with my thoughts, entertain my thoughts, and think my thoughts to be accurate. In the process, my emotions followed my thoughts.

I noticed something about a number of different psychological, philosophical, and spiritual approaches: they pointed to a central reality that our mind causes us the suffering, not the life events. Something happens out there, and our emotional response is due to our thoughts about that event, not the event. Many approaches have arrived at this one conclusion: our thoughts are just that: thoughts. They are about the events, but they are not the events. Just thoughts about them.

Thomas Edison stood and watched his West Orange lab full of experiments and inventions go up in flames. I'm sure he had an initial negative emotional response. But he quickly became excited about the prospects of starting over. He decided this incident provided a fresh start. On the night of the fire, Edison's son Charles looked frantically for his then 67-year-old father. When he found him, Thomas was calmly watching the flames. He suggested getting others to watch, as they would never see a fire like this again. The loss was huge.

The next morning, Edison looked at the ruins and said, "There is great value in disaster. All our mistakes were burned up. Thank God we can start anew."

The same scenario would be a life-long devastation to another person. Either way, the loss is real. Either way, it cannot be undone. But while one person's thoughts might be caught on the loss, Edison focused his thoughts on the possibilities.

Notice that Edison's thoughts are not right or wrong. Neither are the thoughts of the other person. Both are merely thoughts; both lead to an emotional response.

Thoughts are incredibly powerful. They can lead to the heights of creation or to the depths of destruction. Thoughts bring us joy, and they bring us misery. But they are just thoughts, no more real than we allow them to be.

Remember that scale?

Thought   Thought
Reality   Recognition

At one end, we believe a thought that pops into our mind is real. At the other end, we understand the thought is a thought. We recognize it for what it is.

Where on the scale do you dwell? Where do you spend your time?

In order to obey this Immutable Law, we must simply understand, more and more, that a thought is just a thought. It is no more real than we allow it to be. If a thought is helpful, great! Use it. Let it be. If a thought is not helpful, recognize it as a thought and let it pass.

When a thought first hits us, it can feel very real, almost like lenses placed over our eyes. We view the world through that perspective. It hits us and takes control. But the moment I recognize, "This is a thought," I get a little distance from it. Instantly, I am observing myself thinking.

There are two parts to our minds: the thinking mind and the observing mind. Many of us have lost track of the observing mind. So let me bring it back to your awareness.

Have you ever found yourself embroiled in an argument with someone, your mouth and mind engaged, only to have another part of you asking, "What am I doing here? Why am I continuing this argument? I don't really even care about this, and I'm not sure I believe it as much as I keep stating."? If so, you have just experienced your observing mind.

Or perhaps you have tried meditation. (By the way, a central underpinning of meditation is that thoughts no more than thoughts.) The mind creates a thought. You can either follow the thought or return to quiet. Your choice.

That moment when you notice yourself having that thought? Your observing mind was watching your thinking mind. You stepped back to observe your thinking—and perhaps you even managed to let that thought slip away. Or, ironically, you may have become upset, telling yourself "I can't believe I am doing it! There I go, thinking!" At which point, you are once again thinking.

Remember, thoughts are not the problem. Believing them to be real, not just a thought, is the problem.

Once you recognize you are thinking, you get just a little breathing room. In that space, you can take a deep breath, let go of that thought, and discover what happens next: your mood rises. Emotions shape our mood. Thoughts shape our emotions. Release the grip on your emotions, and your mood naturally rises. Hold tightly to your thoughts, and your emotions dip, dragging your mood right down.

Let me be clear: as I write this, I make it sound easy. This is not easy. Simple, yes. Easy, no. Why? Because we live in a world that believes in thoughts. We believe in the reality we build by thinking. Because of this, we have some "thought habits" that are not particularly helpful.

Notice, though, that it does not even have to be a real event causing the lower mood. Do you recall the earlier little "thought experiment" of making yourself angry (or happy, or sad, or any other emotion)? That is accomplished through thoughts. And it happens throughout our daily lives.

The other morning, I was taking my daily walk with my dog. It is my chance to clear my head and get some low-level physical activity to start the day. I neared an intersection and watched a car barely slow for a stop sign as it left my neighborhood. That would be a relatively objective reflection. I then started thinking, "What if someone had been crossing from the right side of the car? The driver glanced to the left, but never looked to the right." At that point, I was thinking. This had not happened. Nobody was crossing the street at that time. It was just a thought. As I continued thinking about it, I found myself becoming angry. I could feel my physiological response to the emotions as a result of my thinking. And then I stopped. I recognized my mood was taking a dive, all due to a thought. It was not about the incident. People do that all the time, not stopping at a stop sign. It was about my thoughts that continued after the event.

It took a few moments to get a little distance from the thought before my mood and physiological state returned to a baseline. All because of a thought.

Notice that this "event" was something small. Nothing significant. Our daily emotional life can be deeply impacted by those little events—or more clearly, our thoughts about those little events. Some days, we can go from one event to another, creating a day full of negative emotional responses to small incidents. For many, that is really the definition of a "bad day." Lots of thoughts about little incidents.

There is an opportunity, as those moments happen, to simply notice your thoughts. An easy way to do this? When your emotions are low, or not where you want them to be, ask yourself, "What am I thinking about?"

This is all about using your "emotional barometer." A barometer is a good measurement of barometric pressure in meteorology. If the pressure is rising, it usually means good weather is coming. If the pressure is dropping, it usually means unstable weather is approaching.

When I am at the beach, I take a look at the barometer in the hall. If the pressure reading is high, we will enjoy the beach. If it is low, we might want to head for the cinemas.

Your emotional barometer is just you taking a reading of your emotional life. If your emotions are higher (joy, contentment, etc.), don't worry about your thinking. If your emotions are low or dropping (angry, resentful, jealous, etc.), it is a good time to ask, "What am I thinking?" Suddenly, you are aware of the thoughts. That brings us back to the Immutable Law, "A Thought Is a Thought."

Once you recognize a thought you are having, you can recognize it is just a thought. Once you recognize it is a thought, you can decide to disengage with it, let it go, let it drop. Or at least simply recognize it is just a thought. A thought is a thought, nothing more.

Building On The Laws

As you continue to move through the Immutable Laws of Living, they tend to build upon one another. When you start moving through one, as you begin to obey that law, prior laws become easier, and further laws have a foundation.

This is especially true with the 4th Law, "*A Thought Is a Thought*." What did you think when you read, "*Life Isn't Fair*" (1st Law)? Did you accept it readily, or did you push back? Did you get a bit upset with the notion that life isn't even about "fair"? That was a thought. The emotional response you had was a reaction to a thought.

The same is true with the 3rd Law, *"Life Isn't About Happiness"*? If you have been chasing happiness, believing life is about happiness, you might have had some thoughts about that chapter. Which may have led you to feel uncomfortable or even angry.

(Remember, I never said you can't be happy and experience happiness. Only that life is not *about* happiness.)

CHAPTER 5

Every Perspective
Is Limited

Have you ever had the experience of watching one of those "news" TV shows? These days, they like to present some crime, focusing on "whodunit." They usually have one prime suspect. During the first part of the show, you are convinced the person is guilty. Then, halfway through the show, they change directions. Toward the end of the show you begin to believe the person is innocent, and by the end of the show, you are completely confused.

What happened during the show?

The simple answer is the producers of the show changed the perspective. They changed their reporting perspective, and it began to affect your perspective. Two people watching the show, by the end, may begin to argue about whether the person is guilty or innocent. And each could support their argument.

How is it possible that two different people can look at the same evidence and arrive at different conclusions?

The same can be seen in politics. As much as one side likes to paint the other as unreasonable, both are viewing the same problems in society. They are also viewing the same resources. And then, they approach the situation from seemingly opposite directions. For the most part, I believe that both sides genuinely want to make society better and solve the big societal problems. Yet, they choose very different approaches.

How is that possible?

We all have a base understanding, a perspective we use to look at the world. There isn't one way of looking at things; there are nearly 7.5 billion ways to look at things. Some may be very similar to each other, but there are differences in the nuance.

We all have a perspective. What we don't like to admit is that every one of those perspectives is limited. We often are able to see the limits of somebody else's perspective, but not many of us are too excited to admit the limits of our own perspective.

In fact, moment-by-moment, we even forget that we're just viewing things from a certain perspective.

To use an overused word, we all have a "paradigm."

A paradigm is a model, a way of understanding something. In reality, it is a shortcut in thinking. We are bombarded by massive amounts of information on a daily basis in our world. Too much information is coming at us too quickly and too often. We have to have a way to sort the information and make sense of it. So, we use our paradigm, our perspective, a mental model, to help us sort through things and make sense of it.

It's not a conscious choice, which is why we forget that we're doing it. It's automatic, and we apply it across the board. There's only one problem: it's not entirely accurate. In fact, a paradigm is relatively inaccurate, but we continue to look for evidence to support it and use that as proof of validation.

We start building our paradigm from the moment we are born. At first, we are trying to figure out whether we can trust or distrust the world. We test to see if others protect us or if we are left to defend ourselves. That begins to be the basis of our perspective. The family in which we grow up also has a group of beliefs. They pass many of those beliefs along to us in stories and lessons.

Our friends have perspectives. Through conversations and stories, they pass along their beliefs (and we do the same to them). We unconsciously pick and choose from these lessons, as they make sense to us. When something doesn't make sense, we pare it away. When something makes sense, we add it into our paradigm (even if it conflicts with other things that "make sense" to us—paradigms are not entirely rational).

Then we go to school where we get lots of different perspectives and information handed to us. We take it in, accept what makes sense, and reject the rest. That process continues through our education and life experiences. It can be shaped by our gender, our religious practices, events in our lives, the people we meet, our socioeconomic reality, and even the time period in which we live.

Without knowing it, we weave these pieces together into a perspective, a way of looking at the world. When a new experience comes along, we don't simply take in the new experience. We judge it through our paradigm. We create a model of reality, rather than experiencing reality directly.

You may have had the experience of watching someone justify the exact same experience you witnessed from an entirely opposite direction. You may be wondering how they could possibly see things the way they are seeing them. Yet if you are with people who see things the way you do, this doesn't happen. You're convinced you see things the way they are.

Every now and then, an experience comes along that completely shifts our perspective. It changes our paradigm.

When I was in college, I had been presented with an individual model of psychology. The whole model was based on how the person, the individual, was formed and created, affected by experiences and internal realities. It was individually focused. Then, during my sophomore year, a professor in the sociology department was teaching a class on family. In that class, he presented a "systems" understanding of families. A systems understanding is based on seeing the interactions of the parts of the system, looking at the functionality of the system. It's based on the dynamics of a group. Suddenly, my eyes were opened. I realized that it was not the individual model that made the most sense, but a systems model.

It changed my paradigm.

Notice that the individual model of psychology is still helpful. But it sometimes removes the individual from the system in which they exist. In fact, many people go to their first psychology class and gain a new paradigm. You may have had that experience. Suddenly, everybody's actions are seen through that understanding. Whatever model it is, you begin to see others fitting into that model, thus validating the truth of that model to you. I had the same experience, several times. Including a new way of viewing it from a systems perspective.

Knowledge and information are always changing our paradigm. An often-noted paradigm shift was when science realized that the earth was not the center of the universe. For a long time, it was believed that the sun was crossing the sky over the earth; the earth was seen as the center of the universe. All the planets, the sun, the stars, and the moon crossed a dome above the earth. Scientists then realized that the earth was round, and believed that these celestial bodies were going around the earth. Then, as more evidence began to emerge, it was realized that the earth was actually going around the sun. And later, science determined that the sun was not even the center of the universe.

At every point, there was a paradigm shift. And whenever your paradigm is shifted, it is very hard to see the old way again.

You probably have experienced this many times in your life. Perhaps you had a certain belief about something or someone. Then you had an experience or interaction, and you realized your belief was incorrect. That old belief likely did not come back. You probably saw it the new way from then on. At least until something else challenged that belief.

Look at politics and social issues. People looking at the same situations and evidence arrive at the opposite conclusions. Usually, we are under the belief that our way of seeing things is the correct one, and others are mistaken.

And that is the problem with this Immutable Law of Living: We All Have a Perspective, and It's Limited.

Paradigms help us crunch the info that is surrounding us into useful information. They allow us to take all the information and use it to navigate the world. The information becomes usable, but that is not the same as accurate. Also, the usability of the information can diminish over time, and in different circumstances.

If you've ever changed geographic locations or even switched groups you are in, you may have noticed that your paradigm, your perspective, is no longer effective. Where you once had lots of agreement, you suddenly find lots of disagreement.

We all tend to stick to our paradigm until it fails us. In fact, we usually desperately hold on to our perspective until it painfully doesn't work. Most of the time, we change paradigms because we're forced to, because the way we see things no longer works.

Every perspective or paradigm shifts over time, usually without us noticing it. Little pieces shift here and there, but we maintain an overall perspective. When the big perspective changes, it usually is abrupt and quite noticeable. Your whole understanding is turned around. It takes a pretty big event to have that happen.

You may even go in search of something that will change your perspective. You might look for a book that helps you understand things differently. You might go to a seminar, hoping to get new tools and understandings. Or perhaps something rattles your perspective, and so you go in search of something that will cause it to make sense. Tragedies, illnesses, and accidents sometimes create the impetus for a change in perspective.

In other words, paradigms and perspectives are malleable. But we don't give them up very easily. Mainly because, in everyday life, we forget that it is perspective and believe it is reality.

Generally, when I am talking with people about this particular Immutable Law, people acknowledge readily that they have a perspective that may not be entirely accurate. People note that others see things differently. So, I may be stating the obvious. But here's the problem: in day-to-day life, people forget this and act as if they are the ones seeing reality. This is the root problem of conflict. When people disagree, they generally dig into their perspective, refusing to acknowledge that they may not be seeing things entirely accurately.

When we are on the top of our game, it's pretty easy to recognize that people see things differently. But, when we are tired or frustrated, when tensions are high and we are engaged in conflict, we forget this. That's where we get into trouble.

How We Disobey This Law

There are three primary ways that we disobey this particular Immutable Law. The ways we disobey this law tend to make us struggle in our own lives and with others.

The first way we disobey this law is by believing that we see things as they are, correctly and accurately. Every perspective has its limits. Every paradigm has its blind spots. When we don't remember this, we begin to believe that we see things as they are.

During my college social statistics class, we examined research to assess whether the research was helpful or limited. We used two measurements: reliability and validity. An experiment was considered to be valid when it tested what it said it was going to test. We looked to see if their method matched what they were trying to do, asking "Was it a valid way of looking at the research?"

Reliability was a different matter. This was more about whether that research could be extrapolated to other situations, or if it was limited to that dataset. Any research had to first be *valid*. But it was generally not useful to a wider audience if it was not also *reliable*.

Paradigms are valid. They take in the information and make sense of it. It's a way of testing and interacting with the world around you. But, paradigms are not reliable. In other words, somebody else could not pick up your paradigm and have it make sense of the world around them. It wouldn't line up for them.

Many times, I will be having a conversation with my wife. I might share some opinion about something. And sometimes, she will note for me that I said one thing, then said another thing, and they are mutually exclusive. And yet, it made sense to me. In other words, it was valid for my view of the world. But it was not reliable for anybody else to use my paradigm. Often, that leads me to re-examine my paradigm.

When we believe we see things as they are, we tend to look for supporting evidence that continues to validate our way of seeing. Social scientists refer to this as *confirmation bias*. We have a natural tendency, a bias, to look for things that confirm what we already believe. In the process, we tend to ignore the things that challenge our current beliefs.

Which leads us to the second way we disobey this law: we resist change, shifts in perspective, and other possibilities. We keep trying to drag our old perspective into new situations, even in the face of mounting evidence that we see things incompletely. You might readily note this in other people, pointing to politicians with outdated views or organizations with no longer efficient approaches. But we all do this. We miss the opportunities of growth and change, for the comfort of relying on our old models.

The reason we do this is because of the third way we disobey this law: we forget we see things from a perspective. We simply forget that we have a paradigm with limits and mistakes. We act as if we see things as they are.

How We Obey This Law

The challenge of paradigms is remembering that we have them. Most people recognize the way they see the world is not complete—until they forget that. And then, people assume that they see the world the way it is, as reality. So, the starting point for obeying this law is to remember that your perspective is limited. After that, it is a matter of trying to broaden your perspective and allow your paradigm to more easily shift to better and more helpful understandings.

Here are four ways to broaden your perspective:

1) Seek out opposing viewpoints. In today's data-feed world, we end up seeing stories that continue to confirm our beliefs. We may not recognize it, but that is the design of social media and the media we choose to consume. Remember that the websites are there to keep you coming back. So, they want to serve you information that you want to read. The basis of information you want to read is information with which you agree. Over time, the curation of the information passed to you more and more matches your paradigm. In other words, the stories you will see in your newsfeed already match your paradigm.

Also, as has become clearer in the past couple of years, every media outlet has a perspective. We tend to seek out the media outlet that agrees with our viewpoint, branding the others as biased and incorrect. They, too, are showing stories that will match their core viewer's paradigm. Their job is to keep you coming back for more so they can sell more advertising.

We have the option, though, to seek out opposing views. We don't seek them out to change our minds as much as to allow our mindset to be challenged—and to think through our own paradigm. Instead of seeing it as binary, "I'm right/you're wrong," it is useful to see that you are viewing it from a different perspective. Let me be clear: you can hold a moral stance and believe that some behavior is wrong. So, we are not talking about everything being relative. It is, however, fair to say that any enduring perspective likely has a point.

Understanding the point being made from other viewpoints is useful in recognizing that your perspective may not be absolutely 100% accurate.

2) Recognize views may be flawed—and flaws are magnified during conflict. In other words, people seem to become more extreme in their viewpoint when there is conflict. Not only do they become more extreme, but they also become more committed. When there is a challenge to a viewpoint, people generally double-down and convince themselves that they are absolutely correct. In times of conflict, it is useful to remember that views *may* be flawed (apply this especially to the views similar to your own).

3) Look hard and hold loosely. Always look for places to stretch. You can be clear about your moral bearings and still look for places that can challenge you and help you to grow. At the same time, you can hold loosely to your beliefs, knowing that they can change. In fact, it's been my observation that people who hold too tightly to their beliefs do so because they fear they are incorrect. People who are secure in their beliefs are willing to hear others' beliefs without having to negate them and allow the beliefs to be a question for them. This does not mean that you are in a constant state of changing your beliefs. Only that you are open to listening and allowing your beliefs to be challenged.

4) Instead of labeling a different perspective as "wrong," recognize that it is a different perspective. Consider how that person may have arrived at that perspective. Consider what might have gone into their own belief structure, even as you think about what went into yours. This is the root of empathy. When you can see where somebody is coming from, and recognize why they are coming from such a perspective, you have built empathy for them. You have also built clarity for yourself.

One of my observations is that most humans want the exact same things. They want to be comfortable, find meaning in life, help others around them, and make sense of the world. We may come at it differently, but we all have the same underlying desires. Many times, we forget this underlying truth, simply labeling the methods as "wrong." But we miss the similarities of where we're trying to go. Many times, as I watch people in conflict, I've been struck by the fact that even though they think they are very far apart, they both have the same underlying desires and hopes. They focus on method and miss the fact that they are connected by their hopes, dreams, and aspirations.

Every perspective is limited. The goal of any perspective is to help you move through life and make sense of the world. It doesn't have to be accurate to do that. With a little space and distance, we have the opportunity of improving the model we use, allowing our paradigm to shift.

CHAPTER 6

Change Is Inevitable

C hange happens.

You don't have to like it, but it's a fact; change happens. Sometimes, the changes are the ones we want. Sometimes, the changes are ones we would rather avoid. But, that's the nature of the world. It's in constant motion: constant change is the rule.

Most people struggle with change. Some people are glad for certain changes, particularly when things have not been going well. They hope for a change that will bring something better. But when things are going our way (or even when things are neutral) most people don't want to change. In fact, change scares most people.

Just the other day, I was having a conversation with a man who was trying to save his marriage. He told me his wife accused him of having changed. He insisted to me he had not changed. He told me he was the exact same way he was when they married. I said, "I hope not. I hope that you have changed in some way over these years. In fact, if you have not changed, you have missed an opportunity. Your life has obviously been changing. You had kids. They grew up. You've changed jobs. Things have happened in your life. If you have not changed, I would be amazed—and saddened for you."

Things change. Life changes. We change. The problem is, we struggle with change. We struggle with the changes around us, and we struggle with making changes. We can't stop the changes around us, so we had better change ourselves in order to keep up.

Sometimes, it depends on whether you're in the driver seat or the passenger seat. In our married life, I tend to be the one who does the driving on trips. My poor wife gets to be the passenger. I recognize that this puts us in very different positions on the trip. From my side of the car, I get to choose how the car is moving, where we're headed, and how we get there. I'm in control. I get to choose. On the other hand, I am also responsible for that car and the passengers in it. From the passenger seat, you are at the mercy of the driver and the vehicle. You have few choices. The driver gets to choose. The passenger has to ride along. On the other hand, the passenger has no responsibility for the safety of the vehicle and passengers.

Change is a bit like that. Sometimes, we are the driver of change—we get to choose change. And we are responsible for those changes. Other times, we are the passenger, at the mercy of changes happening around us. We are not responsible for those changes, but we are responsible for how we deal with those changes.

We like to pretend there is some constant. In reality, the only constant is change. We are in constant flux, surrounded by a world in constant flux.

The planet spins at a rate of approximately 1,000 miles per hour (at the equator), going around the sun at a rate of about 67,000 miles per hour. Our solar system is moving at about 514,000 miles per hour within our galaxy. (And you say you don't travel!)

Depending on where you live, you may experience up to four seasons each year. During those seasons, plants and animals go through constant changes to keep up with climactic change.

We grow older. Our children grow older. Our loved ones grow older. And, in the midst of the aging process, there are unavoidable changes.

In other words, "I don't like change" assumes there is some alternate option, but change is just inevitable. That is the Immutable Law of Living: Change is Inevitable.

How We Disobey This Law

Remember that our mindset about anything shapes how we feel. This is particularly the case with change. Some people have an automatic reaction of "I don't like change." Some people would rather pretend they are not changing and the world around them is not changing. It's tough to hold to this, but many people try.

Which leads to two central ways we disobey this particular Immutable Law.

First, some people simply pretend that nothing is changing. They hide from, deny, and ignore the changes. But think how this impacts life. If you disobey the law in this way, you miss out on all those changes. You could miss out on how the kids are growing up. You could miss out on the interesting ways that change comes into each person's life: health changes, job changes, relationship changes. And if you fall into this category, when you finally DO notice the change, it is a big (and often painful) shift. Children are suddenly off to college. A career ends. Relationships slip away. Health issues that were ignored become huge. This is the cost of pretending that nothing is changing.

The second way we disobey this law is by resisting when we do notice a change—and *need* to change. When we head down this road, we usually keep holding onto old methods and models that no longer work. Or we keep forcing those old models into new situations without seeing the limits.

Did you know that in the early days of trains, many people were struck by them? The tracks would run down the middle of towns, and people would simply step right into the path of the train. They were not used to the sound of a train (as opposed to horse-drawn carriages) and did not expect the train to be moving as fast as it was. Recently, with the advent of electric cars, there was the same issue again. People relied on old models of safety and missed the changes that put them at risk. In fact, manufacturers of electric cars have had to install sounds—the electric engines are nearly silent—so that pedestrians would have a point of reference.

Or how about Uber? Taxi companies have tried to cling to an old model, pretending that nothing is different. But in the new model, everything is different. And by refusing to see the changes hitting that old model, many taxi companies have been scrambling to stay afloat. Their method of dealing with the change? Legal maneuvering to shut down the new model. My guess is this approach will continue to fail. Old models are replaced. Those who cling to the old models find themselves on the losing end.

Notice that refusing to acknowledge a change, and refusing to make an acknowledged change, often leads to the same thing: being stuck, losing out, and paying a high cost.

Since you can't stop change, refusing to acknowledge the change does nothing to stop it. The change comes anyway; the question is whether you keep up, get run over by it, or get left behind.

How We Obey This Law

Since change is inevitable, getting back into obeyance is really simply a matter of dealing with change. First, accept that changes simply happen. Second, decide to at least be okay with change. You don't have a choice on whether they happen, but you do have a choice on your mindset toward them.

How do you get better at change?

Commit to being a lifelong learner. Many times, people leave school and decide they are done with education. Yet, learning is for life. In fact, as you hold this book (or e-reader) in your hand, you are in the process of learning (I hope). We tend to forget all the ways in which we are learning. It may be through reflecting on experiences, reading books and articles, attending seminars, having conversations, traveling to other cultures, or trying new experiences. Accept that this is all about learning and growing. Life is about adapting. You adapt by learning and growing.

Ray Kroc, the founder of McDonald's, once said, "You are either green and growing or ripe and rotting." Commit to being green and growing.

Look toward the edges of your passions, career, interests, and acquaintances. Changes always come from the edges. Those who study paradigm theory note that most innovations come from outsiders bringing a fresh set of eyes and experiences to their fields. Those in the field miss the blind spots. Fresh perspectives bring new possibilities. Keep an eye on the margins.

And remember the other discovery of paradigm theorists: There are three groups in any change. First, there are the "pioneers." They are looking for the new possibilities and potentials. They are the innovators and early adopters. This group loves change. They chase it down and master it. They see the potential of the change, even before it has happened. Second are the "settlers." They follow the pioneers into fairly new areas and use the new resources. They may not love change as much, but they readily see the need to follow changes. They see the potential as the change is happening. Then there are the "resistors." They refuse to go to the "new world." These naysayers are happy to point out why the change is dangerous. They laugh at those who pursue the new opportunities and changes—only to discover they have been left behind.

Don't be left behind. Decide that change is inevitable, and make peace with it. Adapt! Decide to keep growing. You don't have to be a pioneer, but you don't want to be a resistor.

RESOURCE: The Change Matrix

The interesting thing about these Immutable Laws is that many are quite obvious. In fact, as you read them, you may say, "Well, of course." But, the question is whether you follow these laws. In this case, it's a lot like the laws that rule any activity in any country. If you're driving, for instance, there is a speed limit. You may see it very frequently along the highway. That would be the law; it's quite obvious. You may also notice many people do not obey this law.

As we work through these Immutable Laws, my task is to point them out, remind you of them, and help you to understand how to obey them. When I say, "Change is inevitable," it may seem obvious, yet many people struggle to deal with changes.

Let me give you a mental model to think about change. There are two scales involved in any change: horizontal and vertical. When you put these two scales together, you end up with four boxes into which you can place any change.

The first scale is whether the change was desired or undesired. In other words, did you want it to happen or did you not want it to happen? Sometimes things change, and we want them to change. Other times things change, and we don't want them to change.

The second scale is whether the change was expected or unexpected. Sometimes things change, and we see it coming—we expected it. Other times, we had no idea the change was coming—it was unexpected.

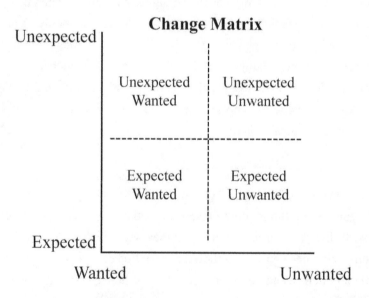

Change Matrix

Unexpected

	Unexpected Wanted	Unexpected Unwanted
	Expected Wanted	Expected Unwanted

Expected

Wanted · Unwanted

The Change Matrix shows that changes happen with four different parameters. Each box contains a different type of change, which is likely to elicit a different response from you.

If a change is desired, but unexpected, you may be delighted by your good fortune. For instance, you receive a windfall. Perhaps a long-lost relative dies and leaves you a small fortune. You may have desired to have more resources, but you didn't expect the windfall. In that case, you will probably adjust to the change fairly quickly.

If a change is desired and expected, you may have looked forward to it with excitement, and prepared for it. For example, if you have been working on a degree, and you get to the point of graduation; it was a desired outcome and expected. In that case, you wouldn't be surprised, but you would be excited.

Whenever a change is desired, we tend to adjust fairly rapidly. That does not mean that the change does not create anxiety. For example, in each of these changes noted above, there could be anxiety attached. If you receive a windfall, you have to figure out how to manage the new money. You may find lots of new friends and struggle to decide on why they want to be your friends. In other words, it may have complicated your life. If you received a degree you had been working on, you are suddenly faced with new opportunities, new possibilities, and new responsibilities. You might have to find a new job.

Even positive changes can create some anxiety.

Then there are the changes that are undesired. These are changes you don't want to happen. Notice that these changes can be undesired by you, but desired by someone else. For example, your children may grow up and leave home. You may not be ready to have them leave so it may be undesired by you. But your children may be more than ready to launch into their own lives. For them, it is desired change.

Or perhaps your spouse decides to leave your marriage, but you don't want a divorce. For you, the change is something you do not want or desire. But that same change is something desired by your spouse.

It may seem that some changes would just be universally undesirable. In most cases, there are those who do desire the change. Some years ago, a huge hailstorm came through my area. It caused a great deal of damage. You can imagine that nobody desired such an event; but fairly quickly, the roofing companies jumped into action. This was exactly the type of storm for which they had been waiting. For many of the companies, it was the opportunity of a lifetime. They had more business than they could possibly serve. I watched little mom-and-pop operations blossom into large companies, all because of an event that (you might imagine) nobody wanted.

Some changes are undesired but expected. For example, you may work for a company that announces it is going to be closing your office in six months. So, while you expect the closure, it isn't anything you want. Generally, we go through a grief process when something is headed our way that we don't want. The anticipatory grief does give us some prep time, but may also leave us anxious during the wait.

Then there are unexpected and undesired changes that all of us experience. The sudden death of a loved one. A diagnosed illness or disease. A tragic accident. These are changes we don't want—changes that catch us by surprise. They may be the most disruptive, with no time to prepare.

The Change Matrix helps you categorize change. There are various types of change, some expected and some unexpected, some wanted and some unwanted. Change isn't just "change," but change comes in various dimensions. And since change is inevitable, our task is to decide how to deal with it.

Whenever a change comes along, remember these four quadrants and place the change into one of those boxes. It helps to clarify your own response to the change and helps to identify the effect of the change. Regardless of the type of change, remember the Immutable Law of Living: Change is Inevitable.

CHAPTER 7

People Do The Best They Can

In all of my years of working with both therapy and coaching clients, I have never had one say, "You know, I am just not doing the best I can. I'm just not trying."

To the contrary, over and over, I have had clients tell me how they keep trying and trying, only to find that they are not making any headway. The issue isn't really about effort, but whether their effort is making a difference. My guess is this is true for you, too.

This doesn't mean that we are always making an optimal effort. I have come to believe one central truth about people: they are doing the best they can, where they are. Let me state that again: People, including you, do the best they can, given their current situation and circumstances, given their perceptions and beliefs, at any moment in time. Sure, in 10 minutes they may be doing something better. They may realize where they're getting stuck. They may read a book, watch something on TV, have a conversation, get some coaching or go to therapy and discover that there is a better way. But in each moment, we all do the best we can.

In fact, this Immutable Law of Living is "People Do the Best They Can (given where they are)."

Unfortunately, we tend to forget this. People are hard on themselves, thinking they should be doing better. People are hard on loved ones, thinking they should be able to get it together. People are hard on strangers, thinking they just don't get it. But the fact is that we all do the best we can, where we are.

We humans often tend to get ourselves into trouble. At those points, we may not be acting optimally, but we are still doing the best we can. Humans often believe their own rationalizations for their behavior and that of others. In fact, we like to believe it so much that we ignore any evidence to the contrary. We tend to over-analyze the situation, adding way too much thought and interpretation to people's actions and reactions to us, and often doubting ourselves.

But that doesn't mean we're not doing the best we can. It certainly means that we are not acting optimally, but humans don't tend to act optimally. Still, we tend to do the best we can, given where we are right now.

So why does this particular Immutable Law matter? It has implications for those around us and for ourselves. When we recognize that everyone is doing the best they can, given where they are, it builds a sense of empathy for other people. While we may not be clear about their motives, and we may not like their actions, it's possible to understand that they have the same struggles as everyone else.

It also allows us to extend self-compassion to ourselves. In other words, instead of chastising ourselves for falling short and not doing our best, we recognize we *are* doing our best. We may still fall short of what we want and expect of ourselves, but we recognize the self-criticism as unwarranted.

So what about when people do bad things? What about when people do mean things? When people mistreat us and others? When they say hurtful things? When they make bad decisions? Does that negate this law?

No.

Generally, people have their reasons for their actions. We may disagree with those reasons, but that doesn't mean they don't have reasons and rationalizations for their actions and behavior. In fact, people do what they do because it seems "reasonable"—at least at the time.

Think about this for just a moment. Isn't it true that every behavior you do, every action comes from some reason in your thinking? It may be that, upon reflection, you realize your reasons were misguided or off-base. You may realize you overreacted or even underreacted. More information or reflection may lead you to understand that your reasons weren't the best. But, at the time, you had your reasons; it made sense to react the way you did.

Let me be clear: this does not excuse all behavior. I do not believe that bad behavior is merely acceptable because somebody has their own reason for the behavior. At the same time, I do believe that people act a certain way because it seems *reasonable to them* at that moment. It may not be reasonable to the people around them, and it certainly may not be reasonable in a court of law. But that does not mean that they had no reason in their own mind.

This is why I believe people do the best they can, where they are. They are acting in ways that seem *reasonable* to them, even if it seems unreasonable to those around them.

It would seem that we humans have a very unique capacity as an organism on this planet. We can fool ourselves as well as others. We are adept at the deception of ourselves and others. This is usually done for self-preservation and/or personal gain, and it's why the behavior seems "reasonable."

How We Disobey This Law

In our day-to-day life, we are quick to judge other people's motives and actions. Sometimes, we are even able to see some of the deceptions in our own motives and actions. We tend to be hard on other people as well as ourselves.

We often expect more (from others and ourselves), and forget that people believe their actions to be reasonable.

We disobey this Immutable Law in three ways.

First, we often act with superiority. We look down upon the actions of others and draw conclusions about their character. Feelings of superiority come from watching from the outside. We are not aware of the internal struggles and rationalizations other people have. We can look at the actions and behavior, and believe them to be unreasonable, all while missing the fact that it is entirely reasonable to the person taking those actions. When we forget this, we build a sense of superiority that is unwarranted. We believe that the other person is not doing the best they can.

Second, we often act with inferiority. When we look at our own actions, we are aware of our shortcomings. When we look at our thoughts, it can lead to feelings of inferiority. We believe that others are doing better, acting better, and not having those same negative thoughts that we have.

The fact is, the human mind is capable of creating an endless number of negative thoughts. We know it from our own thinking, but we fail to notice that others are having the same negative thoughts. It's easy from that perspective to believe that we should be doing better. We forget that we are doing the best we can. If you are on social media, it's easy to see the highlights everyone else shares and compare them with your entire life. It seems to slip our notice that people usually only post the good stuff, the edited version of their lives. At the same time, we live the unedited version of our own lives. That comparison can lead to feelings of inferiority.

Third, when we forget that people do the best they can, where they are, including towards ourselves, we slip into "judgmentalism." Humans are harsh judges of behavior, often missing the internal motivations of others. And when we try to understand those internal motivations, it does not mean we excuse the behavior. Instead, we understand that people take actions for reasons that make sense to them, at that moment. We might have to deal with the behavior and even judge the behavior. That's a bit different than judging the person and the person's motivation. Including your own.

How We Obey This Law

There are several steps in obeying this law.

1) Simply to remember that people really do the best they can, where they are. That gives a little space in understanding other people and ourselves.

When we accept this fact, it naturally moves us to compassion and empathy for other people and ourselves. We tend to understand that everyone struggles and everyone does the best they can. That leads to empathy, and empathy strengthens the compassion.

2) Another way to work through this law is to aim at acceptance. Sometimes, when people are acting in ways that we don't like, we try to rewrite history. We try to ask why things happened and wonder how they could be different. This law points us to accepting what has happened and dealing with "what is" (we will discuss this further in another Immutable Law). This creates the starting point of moving forward. Many times, people get trapped in past events, trying to rework them in our own minds, not so much to understand them as to change them. What happened, how people acted, is what happened. It creates the starting point. Once we have a starting point, we can begin moving forward.

3) Remember to look for "reasonableness" in behavior. Remember that people act in ways that seem reasonable (to them, as they act). We may not agree with their reason, but it makes sense to them. In moments of struggling with somebody else's actions, or your own actions, look for the "reasoning" behind them.

For example, you're driving down the road, and somebody cuts you off. You become angry at their senseless behavior. You can't believe that they would take such action. There is no reckoning in your mind about how they didn't see you and how they can be so reckless. You find your anger rising up. At that moment, it might be tempting to become the aggressive driver, to teach them a lesson. But what if, instead, you recognize that they took an action because it seemed reasonable to them. Perhaps it wasn't the safest of behaviors, but it likely made sense to them. In other words, changing lanes right in front of you seemed reasonable. It doesn't mean the behavior was safe, only that it was reasonable to them. You may notice that this understanding reduces your reactive anger. If you can assume that it made sense to them, that it was reasonable to them, it may keep you from reacting in a way that others would see as unreasonable. At that moment, becoming an aggressive driver may seem reasonable to you, but that doesn't make it safe or helpful.

Finally, this particular law points to an important principle: forgiveness. If you can assume that people are doing the best they can, where they are, it helps in the process of forgiveness. Let me be clear when I speak of forgiveness: I'm not suggesting letting them off the hook, excusing their behavior, or just letting it go. Forgiveness is about releasing the hold someone else has over you, due to their behavior. (You may also apply this to self-forgiveness.)

When you forgive, you release the hold a person's behavior has upon you. You accept that the behavior was hurtful, but you refuse to be held hostage by the hurt. If you understand that the other person was doing the best they can, then it is a bit easier to release the hurt.

(For more information on forgiveness, here is a resource: http://thriveology.com/forgive)

CHAPTER 8

We All Have Fears

I recently read an article about Alex Honnold. Alex is a rock climber who seems fearless in his pursuits. He climbs quickly and efficiently, often without ropes or protection. During a brain scan, scientists discovered that Alex does not have a fear response in the face of his climbing. His brain seems to lack the brain circuitry response for fear that most would experience in a climb.

There are other people, rarely, with damage to the amygdala in their brain. These people seem to have no fear response. Other than those examples, we all have fear.

One might argue that because Alex does not have a fear response, he puts himself in extreme danger. Without fear, he relies on logic and reason to decide whether a move or a climb is risky or something he could attempt. The same is true with those having damaged amygdalae. They may place themselves into overly risky situations without a warning system to let them know.

If you are someone who struggles with fear, it may sound nice to not have to deal with the fear response. The problem is, that fear response keeps you safe. Granted, it may keep you too safe, but that is what this Immutable Law of Living addresses. Perhaps the more helpful action is to stop struggling with fear. Use it.

We all have fears. We all have fear circuitry in our brain. (Except those people noted above.) Our ancestors survived because of this circuitry. It is an automatic response, deep within the most primitive areas of the brain. Imagine your ancestors on the savanna or in the jungles. It would not do them well to ponder a situation that might be risky. A moving shadow, a breeze on the grass, a sound in the distance might all be indications of danger. For survival, it would be better to respond automatically than to have to ponder the situation and assess it.

Those who sat and wondered what the signs might mean would likely end up something's lunch or dinner. Those who used an early warning system, and got out of the way, survived to pass on their genes. We are the recipients of those genes.

We have inherited an early warning system that is hypersensitive and over-reactive. In the dangers of the ancient world, these two were survival traits. In today's much safer environment, these two traits can hold you back. You are likely not reading this book sitting on a rock in the savanna or in a tree in the jungle (if you are, please send me a pic!). Your environment is more likely to be your home, your work, or somewhere in between. And yet, that early warning system is still intact and working to keep you alive, in spite of the fact that predators are very rare in this modern environment.

You can thank your ancestors for surviving and passing on their genes. You can also thank that same process for leaving you with fears and anxiety.

Unfortunately, we tend to use this early detection system and respond as if there is a threat behind every corner. We have come to listen to fear as a warning to avoid. The problem is, new situations and anxious situations both trigger a fear response. But it's possible that at the end of a new situation or an anxious situation, there is something good. For instance, you are asked to give a speech at work. Your immediate reaction is a fear response. You don't like to speak in public, and you don't know what you would say. You wonder what people will think. You think about the mistakes you might make. (I say this because many people have fears of speaking in public.) But what if, at the end of that speech, there were opportunities not available before the speech? A new opportunity, a pay raise, a new position, all because of a speech—a speech that is likely NOT a real threat to your physical survival.

If you were to let your fear hold you back, you would miss the opportunity. As far as I have been able to ascertain, nobody has died from public speaking. Nobody has been eaten for lunch or dinner over a speech, even when the speech included a pretty bad chicken meal. It just feels that way, because of that fear circuitry. If we believe the fear, we avoid the speech, believing it to be a threat to our well-being.

Let's try to divide fears into two categories: Protective Fears and Existential Fears.

I love to trail run. It puts me in the middle of the woods, away from traffic, surrounded by peaceful nature. Well, usually peaceful nature, at least where I run. But as I'm running down the trail, I see a squiggly thing on the ground. My fear response brings me to a sudden halt. It keeps me safe, in case that squiggly thing ends up being a snake. Honestly, in all but one instance, it has ended up being a stick. Still, that protective fear keeps me safe, even at the risk of being too safe.

If you're walking through a city, you may see an area that scares you. It's possible that it should scare you. And because of that fear response, you avoid it. Perhaps nothing would've happened, but your fear circuitry made sure nothing happened by having you avoid that area.

While our world is much safer than that of our ancestors, it is not sterile. There are still risks, and your brain is trying to keep you safe. In fact, there is not much we can do to keep you from having an immediate fearful response. Once you decide that a situation is safe, you can continue, like I do on the trail. But that immediate response kicks in automatically.

When our children were small, we were visiting the Grand Canyon. I spent more time worrying about my children stumbling over the edge than looking at the view. My fear response included my loved ones and wanting to make sure that nothing happened to them. Given their age, it seemed possible that they could stumble right over the edge. So I stayed on alert, as did my wife. That is the nature of protective fear. It won't go away, even if it is overactive.

The nice thing about protective fear is that once you understand it, you know you just need to assess the situation and decide on your actions. If I see a squiggly line down the trail, I don't have to turn around and go back; I don't have to quit trail running. I simply have to gather more information and make sure the situation is safe.

Existential fears are a different category. We all have these existential fears. Some of us feel the fear more than others, but all of us live with them.

There are three distinct existential fears:

1) I won't have enough
2) I won't be loved enough
3) I won't be good enough

If you are familiar with Maslow's Hierarchy of Needs, you will notice that these fears fit into the various levels. The most basic need, according to Maslow, is the need for basic necessities. This includes food, water, shelter, and safety. These are also our issues around this existential fear of "I won't have enough." These needs are very real. But, for most people reading this book, it is a fear, not reality. You likely have enough to eat and drink, have shelter, and are safe. That doesn't mean, though, that this fear is abated. As an existential fear, it creeps in anyway. In fact, this fear creates a scarcity mentality. It can make you feel like there's not enough, even when there is. It can make you concerned that there might not be enough.

This fear can keep you up late at night, or wake you early in the morning, worried about your resources. If you find yourself concerned about money, for instance, this is the fear that is activated. To be clear, it is possible for this fear to be true. It is possible to not have enough. However, many times, this fear is activated when it is not necessary. This fear rears its ugly head in the face of both plenty and scarcity. One important note about this fear: even when there truly is a scarcity or shortage, the fear does nothing to fix the situation. Having the fear does not change the reality—unless a change is made in some way.

In the middle layers of Maslow's hierarchy, the concern is about belonging. It is about having a partner, a family, a tribe, a community. It is about being a part of a larger group, of being important to somebody. Again, this fear may not match reality. You may have a spouse who loves you, a family who loves you, or a community that loves you, and still have this fear that you won't be loved enough.

Sometimes, when people are having a relationship problem, this fear creeps in. It can feel like that relationship holds all of the "love needs." Even though there are plenty of others loving you, that one relationship can trigger this fear. Remember that it is rare for somebody to lack in any loving relationship. And the vast majority of us have multiple loving relationships around us. In the moments of this fear, there are still likely many people loving you and wanting the best for you. But again, having this fear does little to change reality.

At the top of Maslow's hierarchy is self-development. The very top is self-actualization, and just below that, it is about competency. That third fear, "I won't be good enough," is at this level. Notice that the statement is open-ended; it does not specify the area over which you are good enough. It is overarching. The feeling of not being good enough can extend into many areas of life: career, hobbies, athletics, relationships, or any other area. You can doubt your competency in any number of areas.

These three fears, the existential fears, are the ones that keep you up at night, wake you up in the middle the night, or grab you in the morning. The protective fears are triggered by an event. The existential fears are likely to be triggered by your imagination, your thoughts. Nothing has to necessarily happen for you to be gripped by these fears (by which, I mean, nothing external has to happen—which is different than your internal imaginings of things happening).

Our culture has fallen in love with the word "stress." In reality, stress is not something outside of you. It is your internal response to something outside of you (or imagined outside of you). Stress is really a different word for fear. Often, the stress we feel is tied to an existential fear. For example, too much is coming your way (at least in your perception), and it triggers your fear of not being good enough. Upheaval at work may feel like a threat to your job. This could cause a fear of not having enough. A relational issue in your life, leading to conflict or difficulties, can raise the fear of not being loved enough.

We tend to focus on how to "cope with stress." Often, this is about avoiding the "stressful" thing. The real issue is how to deal with these fears. Attempts at calming the stress, or de-stressing, miss the point that stress is really fear. Let's call it what it is so we can deal with it directly.

Being human predisposes us to fear. Our capacity for thinking and imagining creates these existential fears. And these fears can sometimes get in the way of living a thriving life.

How We Disobey This Law

Most people don't like to admit to fear. It can make us feel weak or flawed. So, we use lots of other words to describe it. Like stressed, worried, or anxious. In reality, they are all just words for fear. It was okay as a child to admit to fear. You could fear the boogeyman or some other imaginary creature, and it was okay. Back then, adults tried to assure you that there was nothing to fear. Then somewhere along the way, it stopped being okay to be fearful.

The first way that we disobey this law is by believing that fear is somehow wrong. By believing fear is somehow wrong or cowardly, we either deny fear or chastise ourselves for having fear.

Fear is deeply wired into our brains. While it may not be helpful in your life, at least in the way it's working now, fear is not wrong. Fear just is. Also, fear has nothing to do with being weak or flawed or cowardly. There is no association between being fearful and being weak. And fear is certainly not a flaw. It is a survival mechanism. Admittedly, our fear response is too sensitive, but it has served to get your genetic makeup to this point and into you.

Which leads to the second way that we disobey this law: we believe that we are the only ones who have fear, as individuals. Oh sure, with a little reflection we realize that others have fear, too. But in the moment of fear, we either imagine that we are the only ones feeling it or become so focused on our own feelings that we believe it is only us. So, let me assure you that everyone feels fear. (What they do with it, that's another question.)

The final way that we disobey this law is the most important. We allow fear to keep us from acting. Or at least from acting in the way we really want to. We let fear deter us from moving in the direction we want to go.

If you believe that fear is telling you that something is dangerous, then it makes sense that you would allow it to deter you. Right?

But what if that is not the case? What if that is not the role of fear?

Fear is not a deterrent emotion. It is only pointing out that something is important. Many people use fear as an Avoidance-Indicator. In other words, fear points out things to avoid. As an Avoidance-Indicator, fear is used to stay away from things. For example, some people have told me about things they wanted to do. When I asked why they had not done them, they replied, "Because I was afraid." In other words, their fear was their reason for not taking action.

How We Obey This Law

Obeying this law requires a shift in your relationship with fear. The shift is not difficult, but can transform how fear works in your life.

1) Make fear an indicator of importance. Let me suggest that there is a better use of fear. Instead of it being an Avoidance-Indicator, fear is an Importance-Indicator. Fear is simply pointing out that something is important and needs attention. It is simply asking for our alertness. Not avoidance, but alertness. A major way of obeying this law is by using fear to indicate importance. When you feel fear, it is an alert to pay attention because something is important.

For example, let's say that you are at a gathering. You look across the room and see somebody that you think might be interesting to talk to. Just somebody interesting. You may feel a little bit nervous about approaching them, but no big deal. But what if you were looking for the love of your life? And you looked across the room, seeing someone you think might be "the one." My guess is, your anxiety level would be much higher. Your fear would kick in. But your fear is not telling you to avoid that person. Your fear would simply be telling you that this is important; your fear is alerting you to the fact that this person might be important. You don't want to stay away from the person who could be "the one." Otherwise, they never become "the one."

If I were to ask you why you did not approach that person (assuming you did not approach the person), you might tell me that it was because you were scared/anxious/nervous. Your reason for not approaching that person would be about feeling the fear. And yet the fear was telling you how important it was to approach that person.

Or perhaps you are looking for a new job and you have two job interviews. The first one is a job that you could do but don't particularly want. The second would be your dream job. It would challenge you, compensate you, and be a job you could see yourself in for years. In the first job interview, you don't feel any anxiety and are relaxed. In the second interview, you're sweating and nervous. At the end of it, you walk away feeling unsure of yourself. Some people would grab that first job because it was comfortable. They might even take it as a sign or confirmation, since they were not anxious during the interview. In reality, the second job was the important one. And the reason for the fear was because of the importance.

We obey this Immutable Law of Living (We All Have Fears) when we use fear as an Importance-Indicator.

We first use fear to point toward something important. Which leads to the next step.

2) Act courageously. Courage is not a lack of fear; it is acting in spite of fear. Years ago, when my son was a young Cub Scout, I was helping lead an activity in his pack. The boys were talking about an incident they heard about that had something to do with firefighters. They were talking about the courage of the firefighter, so I asked them what they meant by courage. All agreed that the firefighter who took action hadn't had any fear. I suggested to them that if you have no fear, it isn't courageous. It is just acting. Courage comes when we take action *in spite* of fear.

One important skill is the capacity of soothing yourself in the midst of fear. Many times, when lots of things are happening at the same time, people tend to allow themselves to be overwhelmed. Sometimes, fear is cumulative. You can take action when fear is just intermittent, here and there. But when it starts stacking up, you can get overwhelmed. The fear begins to take a toll and is harder to address.

Think of it as a measuring cup. If you are constantly able to pour off some of the ingredients, the cup won't be a problem. But if you just keep heaping ingredients in, eventually, it will overflow. Once it is overflowing, it isn't much use. If you allow the fear to fill you up, you may find yourself stuck in fear mode.

3) Take care of yourself, physically. One way to keep the cup from constantly filling is to make sure you are taking care of your body. It will be more capable of dealing with fearful situations as they arise if you do. Remember that fear creates a bodily response (your entire body is involved in any fear response). In the days of our ancestors, the moments of fear were acute—a lion or enemy suddenly appears. Then, the threat would pass, and people could return to calm. Today, our fear-provoking issues are chronic. You might have to face that same angry boss or disagreeable co-worker every day. You may spend every month finding ways to stretch your check to cover all the bills. The "stimuli" are more chronic than acute. That means your biological systems are more constantly taxed.

If you are well-rested and well-nourished, you are better equipped to deal with the issues. If you are exercising, you are also burning off some of that adrenaline flowing through your system. Remember that a fearful moment for our ancient ancestors was likely followed by (or included) a sprint from danger.

Be sure and take care of your body. (See my Thriving Body Podcast Series: http://thriveology.com/thrivingbody)

4) Breathe (correctly). There is another little "biology hack" you can use when you find your fear response on the rise. Since both protective fears and existential fears end up activating your brain's fear system, you can use this technique for both categories.

The primitive fear part of your brain is so ancient, it doesn't understand words. It focuses on sensory input. And it is tightly tied to the body's response system. So, you can't just talk to it and calm it. Not that it won't listen—it just can't understand the words!

There is another input it DOES understand, and over which you have command (when you choose). You may have not noticed, but while you were reading this book, you were breathing. You didn't have to think about it, it just happens. It's part of the survival wiring of your brain. But, now that I have drawn your attention to it, notice you can *choose* how you breathe. You could choose to inhale … now. And you could choose to exhale … now. In other words, while it operates automatically, you can take over control when you want to.

Breathing is a feedback loop to your brain's fear response. When you feel threatened, you automatically begin to breathe with your chest. Your stomach muscles tighten to protect your rather vulnerable internal organs; you are readying for a fight (even if the fear response was about nothing requiring a fight). If you were to breathe deep into your diaphragm, your brain would get a clue. This is basically telling your brain, "All's clear." Automatically, in response to fear, the breathing goes to chest breathing. When calm, it naturally goes to diaphragmatic breathing. Except for the fact that we have been taught to "stand up straight and hold in your gut." Thus, we restrict our diaphragm. Partly, that is constantly sending a clue to the brain that there is a threat. No wonder we all have such a quick trigger!

Notice how a baby breathes. They know how to do it! A sleeping baby breathes through the diaphragm. Their little tummies go up and down. It's automatic to the baby. We unlearn that along the way.

But you can relearn it. To get in touch with your diaphragm again, lie down on a flat surface and put a hand over your belly button, the other hand over your chest bone. Work to breathe in such a way that only the hand on your belly button rises. The hand on your chest should remain still. The reason you do it lying down is so you can see the difference. But once you get it, you can do it while standing, sitting, or lying down.

When you notice you are feeling fear (anxious, worried, scared, stressed— whatever word you choose to describe it), belly breathe. (One method is called Box Breathing. Learn more here: http://thriveology.com/breathe)

Focus on your breaths and notice your anxiety begin to dissipate. Perhaps not to zero, but to a more manageable level, which then gives you room to choose your action.

Which leads us to the final way to obey this Immutable Law:

5) Raise your tolerance to fear. Fear pretends to protect you. It acts like a friend, "Don't do this. It is dangerous. Stay clear." Fear is no friend. It may be able to advise you to pay attention. That is the proper role for it.

Don't let fear tell you what to do. Take in the advice that something is important, then choose your own response. You may say, "That is unsafe, and I choose to avoid it." You may also say, "Yes, I feel fear, AND I choose to take action." Fear is just one of the advisors. Purpose and Passion are two other advisors, at least as important. Listen to them and then choose your response.

The more you refuse to allow fear to call the shots, the higher your tolerance to fear. When you give in to it, you embolden fear. It knows it has your ear. So, fear begins to close down more and more of your life, pretending it is "keeping you safe." Instead, you just end up living small.

Act in spite of fear (courage), and you starve it, you reduce fear's power, and your life enlarges.

By feeling fear, noticing what is important, and choosing to act, you raise your tolerance to fear. You are better at it the next time. You build your "courage muscle" and reduce the power fear holds.

Fear. Everyone has fears. Some recognize the fear is only pointing out importance, not avoidance. Move into life, in spite of fear.

CHAPTER 9

Your Life is YOUR Responsibility

E very now and then, I see a certain bumper sticker that says, "Don't blame me. It's not MY fault." Generally, the basis of the sentiment is a political view that is counter to the person elected. But what I really notice is the whole issue of blame and fault. We are a culture rooted in those two words.

We want to assign blame, find who is at fault, and hold others accountable. And in the process, we end up missing an important Immutable Law of Living: Your Life is YOUR Responsibility.

A few years back, I had a client who was pretty successful in his financial life. His bank account was full, and he lived a pretty big life—large house, big boat, lots of toys, lots of vacations, and big watches. But his story in my office was pretty much a country song: "Everybody done me wrong." He told me how his friends took advantage of him, got mad at him, and deserted him. His spouse (soon-to-be-ex, and number 3) was cheating him out of money. She was mad at him and was deserting him. His parents, he surmised, had not given him the parenting and love he needed. Now, they were mad at him and didn't have much to do with him. His kids took him for everything he had, then wanted nothing to do with him. His company was stealing money from him. His workers were cheating him out of a decent day's work. And he was not particularly welcome in his own business.

I stopped him and asked, "What is the one thing all those situations have in common?"

He paused, but only for a second, and told me, "Oh, I see. The world screws you!"

"Nope," I responded. "The one common feature in all of those stories is YOU."

My client stared at me, took that in, and said, "So, you think this is all MY FAULT?"

As kindly and gently as I could, given his wounded expression, I said, "I really am not pointing out blame, but I am pointing out the fact that you are the common link in all those situations. You are the one responsible for choosing how to address the problems. I have no idea, nor any care, as to who is at fault. But I am keenly interested in how you stop blaming everything and everyone else, and how you choose to respond. If you want better relationships, you may want to look at your response. If you are upset about business, you may want to look at how you respond."

Responsibility. Tough word. It is, really, "Response-Ability." It is the ability to respond. We humans have the ability to choose our response. We aren't locked into instinctual reactions. We don't have to let our emotions choose our actions. We can decide how we want to respond.

Your life is YOUR responsibility. How your life goes. What you do in your life. What level of "success" or "happiness" you experience. How you live out your inborn design. All are your responsibility. I believe we are designed to live a life of purpose, find deep meaning, and make an impact. It is the responsibility of each person to discover their purpose, meaning, and impact within the constraints of their life.

As a corollary to this law, others are responsible for their lives. You can't do it for them. You can't make them happy (although you do have the capacity of making someone else pretty miserable). And you can't keep them from making bad decisions (a painful discovery for most parents).

This does NOT mean that all the bad things that might happen to you are your fault. In fact, this law has nothing to do with blame or fault. It has to do with the capacity of each person to choose a response, given the current situation. There are some pretty unavoidable things in life: the situation you are born into and the fact you will die. In between, we have lots of options for responding. Along the way, life gives us obstacles with which we must deal. How we deal with opportunities and obstacles—that is entirely our responsibility.

So, all the bad things that happen to you—not your fault. All the good things that happen to you—not solely because of you. How you respond to both, that is entirely your responsibility.

Also, this law does not mean "every person for themselves." We don't come into the world on an even playing field. Just by the genetic crapshoot, some have more options and opportunities. Part of our responsibility is seeking justice for those who have fewer opportunities. That is part of the impact we can make in the world. We are "response-able" to make this world more hospitable for all. It is then up to each person to decide how he/she will respond.

Many times, we get the whole "responsibility" question wrapped up in "fault." I'm not really talking about fault at all here. It is simply the fact that each one of us is responsible for how we move through the world, given our surroundings. "Fault" is really just looking for something/someone to blame.

If you are standing in the middle of a burning house, the flames licking up the walls, you would be poorly served to ask, "Who did this? Whose fault is it that the house is on fire?" It would be a wise moment to ask, "What do I need to do to get myself, and anyone else I can help, out of this house?" That is the difference between fault/blame and responsibility. Given a situation, responsibility is deciding how to respond, not who to blame.

Viktor Frankl was an Austrian neurologist and psychiatrist. He also survived the Holocaust (and concentration camps), losing his wife and other family members to the Nazi's. Frankl believed before his imprisonment that people are motivated by meaning. During his imprisonment, Frankl became convinced of this, watching the laboratory of real life.

In his book, *Man's Search for Meaning*, Frankl writes, "Between stimulus and response there is a space. In that space is our power to choose our response. In our response lies our growth and our freedom." When we react, we pretend this space does not exist. When we choose a response, we expand that space and live within it. From making that space, we grow and gain freedom.

Every day, we are presented with choosing either reaction or response. We are faced with throwing up our hands in defeat or looking for another path.

Perhaps a business owner is watching a business fall apart. That owner has the option of finding a different path (either with or without the business) or following the business down in flames.

Or a person in a troubled relationship can continue down the path of relational pain and hurt. There is the option of choosing a different path, either by improving the relationship or ending it.

Maybe a person realizes his or her health is failing. There is the option of continuing down the decline or finding a different response. I once had an overweight and out-of-shape person tell me, "What's the use? I'm going to die someday, anyway." I agreed and added, "The question is really how you choose to live until then." This is the question we all must face (or duck).

How We Disobey This Law

There are four ways we disobey this Immutable Law (Your Life Is Your Responsibility):

1) Many times, people proclaim something is "Not My Fault." In that switch from responsibility to fault, they are giving up all responsibility,

deciding to critique and criticize from the sideline. But, life is not so much about fault—deciding who to blame—it's more about looking for where to accept or claim responsibility.

2) Another similar approach is to say, "There is nothing I can do." In some situations, there is nothing to do directly that would change the process. But we always have a choice in attitude. Many disobey the law with despair, believing there is nothing that can be done, externally or internally. However, if I can't change something, I can always change my attitude toward it.

3) This law is also disobeyed by proclaiming someone else is to blame. This is really a link with the other two. If it is not my fault, it must be someone else's fault. And therefore, I can't do anything. The real problem is this: when we decide it is not our fault and we begin to look for someone else to blame, we stop looking for responses. We stay in a blame-frame. Let's be clear that this is, again, not about shifting to self-blame. It is really about avoiding the blame frame.

4) Another way to disobey this law is to refuse to choose (and refusing to see that even *that* is a choice). When I was a child, my father returned from a trip with the gift of a paperweight. On the granite was black lettering that read, "Not to Decide Is to Decide." In other words, even when we refuse to choose (maybe even pretending there is no choice), we are making a decision. No decision is still a decision.

How We Obey This Law

In order to obey this Law, we must first be clear about what the law means. I am not saying that you create everything in your life (good or bad). There are outside forces acting upon us. There are limits to our capacity to change things. But given where we are and what is happening, it is up to us to accept responsibility on how we move forward.

We get to choose our path, but not the starting point. Where we go—given the opportunities and paths presented—is up to us.

I do not believe that you cause everything in your life. That is not the point of this Immutable Law. Where you are born, your genetic makeup, actions taken by those in power, those are the starting points to your journey, the "givens." Options in life comprise the paths presented to you. It is up to you to choose which paths you follow.

What about those times when it would seem there is no action you can take, nothing you can do? Viktor Frankl again guides us here, stating, "Everything can be taken from a man but one thing: the last of the human freedoms—to choose one's attitude in any given set of circumstances, to choose one's own way." He adds, "When we are no longer able to change a situation, we are challenged to change ourselves."

How do we step into response-ability? Let me suggest a few ways.

1) Look for common recurring themes in your life. Look for the places where you seem to be playing "Groundhog Day," repeating the same scenarios. Maybe there are different people, but it seems to roll out the same way, with you playing the same role. Maybe it is around conflicts. Or perhaps health issues. Or it could be work situations, relationship issues, or familial struggles. Just look for the places where you seem to be caught in a very familiar loop.

What was your role in each of those situations?

What was the choice you made that created the loop?

How might you make a different choice the next time? (And there *will* be a **next time**.)

2) Make a shift from *reactive* to *proactive*. While this is not always possible, it makes a huge difference. The more we address on the front end, the less we have to address on the back end.

For example, several years ago, my children and I ate lunch at a restaurant on one of their school holidays. As I remember, they were out of school that day, and it was going to be my chance to visit with them before they caught up with friends. We had a nice lunch and walked outside to my car—only to find my car was dead. Not even one of those "click-click" sounds. I called Roadside Assistance, and they told me they would be there in an hour or so. My kids were stuck with me—at least until their friends could make it and pick them up. Roadside Assistance said the battery wasn't the problem, so, we had to be towed to the dealer. That was another delay. One of my daughter's friends took us home, and my son then went his way with a friend.

To say it was not the day I had imagined would be an understatement. In the end, the dealer discovered the battery was defective. Not my fault. Nothing I could do. Just bad luck. Except—I remembered, several times in prior weeks when I got in the car and turned the key, it did not immediately turn over. When I tried again, it started. "No big deal," I would say to myself. But it was. Had I been proactive and taken it in when it was giving me some clues, I would not have been stranded (nor would my kids), having to have it towed in. Proactive would have saved me from reacting.

The same is true with our health, relationships, work, and many other areas. We can either take care of it on the front end or have a bigger mess on the back end. If you ignore your health long enough, there will be issues later.

Being proactive will not prevent everything. Cars still break down. People still get sick. But if you can reduce the number of potential issues on the front end, you have less to figure out when life is coming at you. It just lowers the number of issues you must respond to later.

3) Accept and assume full responsibility for your own life. Just decide that if it is in your life, happening to you, it is your responsibility. (Again, not fault, but response-ability.) One of my colleagues, Jack Canfield, suggests a formula to understand:

E + R = O

The formula states that "Event + Response = Outcome."

The "Event" is anything external to you, over which you have no control. It could be the actions of another person, a natural disaster, or some other event. It may be huge or small. If you can't control it, that is the event. For many people, the "Event" equals "Outcome." It happens, nothing can be done, so that is that.

The "Response" is your choice. It is how you act (and at times, how you choose not to act), and is under your control—even if you don't always see it as your choice). That response may be a myriad of actions on your part to deal with the event. It starts with assuming it is your responsibility to choose how you deal with an event.

The "Outcome" is what happens in combination of the event and your response. And note that it *is* the combination; the event does not force the outcome. Neither does your response. Both are important. You cannot fully choose the outcome—only your response. But your response is an important part of the outcome.

Accepting full responsibility for your life is knowing that when events come your way (things outside of your control), you have the opportunity of choosing your response. When you choose your response, you affect the outcome. (I highly recommend Jack Canfield's book, *The Success Principles*.)

And finally, your responsibility for your life is for just that: *your* life. You must also allow others to be responsible for their own lives. While parents do have some responsibility to protect their (young) children, other people must take responsibility for themselves. Some people will try to get you to be responsible for them. That is a losing proposition. You will have responsibility, but no power; and they get to play the role of victim. This is a losing proposition for all involved.

This is not so much about forcing responsibility on others, as it is realizing you must let them be responsible for their own lives. This is less about abdication of your role and more about clarification of your role in others' lives.

CHAPTER 10

What Is IS What Is

"It is what it is." Have you heard people say that? Usually, I hear it less as acceptance and more as defeat. Usually, after struggling with something, someone says, "Well, it is what it is." Many times I have noticed it is not even the person struggling who says it, but a bystander.

What I notice is people actually DO struggle with "What Is." In fact, that may be the root of more issues in therapy and coaching than anything else. It is probably the biggest factor that gets people stuck—and keeps them stuck.

The ancient Western mythologies believed in the Fates. These three women controlled the destiny of everyone. One would spin the thread of life, another would measure the span of life, and the other would cut the thread. Humans had no choice. No escaping. It was a "fatalist" approach to life. The Fates chose destiny, and humans were more or less puppets of this destiny. There's no changing what is to happen.

Today, we have less of a "fatalistic" view, most of us believing we do have at least some choice in our destiny (especially if you follow the prior Immutable Law on responsibility). But we might just want to adopt a "Reverse Fatalism" view. What if we were to decide or realize that "what has happened has happened—there is no changing what has happened"?

We struggle with that. As a hospital chaplain, I watched people struggle with illnesses and accidents on a daily basis. Many times they asked, "Why?" I came to realize they were not looking for an explanation of why the accident occurred or the illness struck, but *how*. Or, more accurately, "How could we have this NOT happen?" They were looking for a way to undo or redo what had happened.

And yet, it had happened.

As a therapist, people often tell me stories about what happened to them, making them who they are. It is basically a telling of the "origin story" of their struggle. But what I realize is, many times, they are looking for some way to undo it. They tell the story looking for some missed angle or space to change what had happened.

And yet, it had happened.

As far as I can tell, we humans are uniquely gifted and cursed with the capacity to reflect upon events in the past. We have the capacity to think through the (imagined) factors around the event—the thoughts and motivations of others, the reasons for the events, and the meaning behind the events. We have a harder time accepting "What Is" and letting it go.

And so, we become anchored to those events—even as we try to undo or redo them, searching for some way they would not have happened. We struggle to accept "What Is."

Many people have bought into a belief that life is (or should be) a steady, even process of progress. If you graph it, the line should run consistently from the lower left to the upper right side of the graph. Life simply improves along the way. Thus, any deviation from that is seen as wrong. Which means that when something happens that we would rather not have happen (illnesses, accidents, struggles, difficulties, bad relationships, etc., etc.), we have a hidden belief it should not be "that way." We struggle, then, with those bad things, with "What Is."

In reality, life is an up-down, up-down, squiggly, detouring path across the graph. That's the nature of life—for everyone. And at the end? It ends. For everyone. The question is not so much how squiggly that line is, but how we live through that crazy, twisted, turning line of life.

Which is only complicated as we struggle to accept "What Is."

How We Disobey This Law

Whenever we find ourselves trying to rewrite or remake history, we are fighting against "What Is." Sometimes, people just refuse to see the evidence of where they are, choosing to avoid their situation. When we refuse where things are, we disobey this law.

You might call this denial. At its root is a refusal of "What Is." I've watched people in broken and failing relationships continue on as if nothing is happening. They keep acting as if everything is fine with the relationship, yet all signs point to the fact that it is slowly choking and sputtering to destruction. And here is the sad thing: many of those marriages could have been saved if the situation had been clarified and addressed earlier.

It happens with our health. Before my body gave me my "wake up call," I was out of shape and overweight. At some level, I knew this. But I pretended it was not the case. I refused to notice the pictures I now see and know should have been "wake ups." I refused to pay attention to the ever-larger sizes of clothes I needed ("Just a tighter fit," or "Just want a looser fit"). I refused to pay attention to feeling tired and bad. I just kept getting up and repeating the days. Along the way, my body was paying a higher and higher price—until it broke.

When we choose to ignore the evidence (consciously or unconsciously), we disobey this law. When we deny what is happening to us and around us, we disobey this law.

But related to this is the belief held by some that looking at "What Is" really is pessimism. It isn't. Pessimism is the belief that things cannot get better, moving forward. Seeing "What Is" is not pessimism. It is the starting point of your path. Being clear about "What Is" only sets the beginning point of the rest of your path.

Let's say you have decided to explore the woods. You know there is a path through the woods. It meanders through the forest, going up and down the hills, around the bogs, twisting and turning as it goes. You know that if you follow the path, you will arrive on the other side of the forest.

Off you start on the path. Things are going well. But as it gets darker and darker, as you take turns along the way, and as the forest encroaches more, the path is a bit harder to find. At some point, you are no longer sure about the path. At that point, you could simply continue to wander, pretending you are still on the path. But that will likely only cause you to be more lost, further from points of reference. Or you could pause, assess the situation, and pull out the map. You might use that map as a way of assessing where you are. Once you have figured out where you are, you know where to go. If you just wander, it is not about "going" anywhere, as much as it is about wandering and hoping. Progress through the woods comes from knowing where you are and where you are headed. Where you are? That is "What Is." That's your spot on the map.

Another way we disobey this law is by trying to rewrite history. Sometimes, people want to make things "not happen." We spend time trying to rewrite events. I say "trying" because it takes lots of energy with little results. It can come in big and little ways. When we play the "If Only" game, we are proposing how it could have gone differently, which would have placed us at a different spot. "If only that person had not gotten in that car," "If only that person had seen a doctor," "If only I had not made that trip," "If only I had taken that job," and an infinite list of other "If only's."

In the process, we miss "What Is," and the starting point of dealing with it. Energy goes into alternate realities, not the reality that is. Since, as far as we can tell at this moment, it is impossible to go back and do a "redo," "If Only" is simply a mental exercise, or wishful thinking. It changes nothing, but it does keep you chained to that event. Oddly, the anchor point is the event you keep trying to change.

Which leads us to the worst side-effect of violating this law: it traps you in the role of victim. If you believe something else could have and should have happened, then what happened is seen as unfair. This causes a person to have a victim mentality. Sometimes, we *are* victims. But that is different than getting caught in the role of victim. Once we adopt the role it is not an occurrence, but an identity. A victim of an event can choose how to move forward, given what happened. A victim mentality keeps the person anchored to that event, unable to move forward to a new future.

How We Obey This Law

"What Is" can be a struggle. But the bigger struggle is when we refuse to accept "What Is." As humans, we are all masterful writers of fiction—in our own lives. So, we keep writing and rewriting, trying to edit out what we don't want to have happened.

When you are struggling, trying to make what *has* happened different (versus trying to make things different moving forward), stop and ask, "What Is?" Assess the difference between "What *should have* happened" and "What Is or what *did* happen." Whatever happened, once you accept "What Is," you can begin to decide how to respond and how to move forward. But until you accept "What Is," there is no way to move forward—"forward" is not even defined unless you know your starting point. No map is useful until you know your starting point.

If you find yourself struggling, look for where you are refusing "What Is." Or maybe you aren't quite "refusing," but trying to "redo" what happened. Not "do differently" but to "RE-do" what has already been.

To be clear, struggling against things is different than having a tough time—or even having tough or terrible things happen. Bad things happen in every life. Struggling against those tough things is the bigger issue. Refusing to admit what happened has happened, that is the struggling.

I've noticed a proliferation of "Happiness" books in the last decade or so. That tells me people want to experience happiness. But for many people, "happy" comes from external forces. Something has to happen *before* you can be happy. And in fact, "happen" and "happy" share a loanword from Norse history: "hap." That word described fate or chance—something externally occurring. Something has to "happen" to you to make you "happy."

In my experience (and in the teachings of many Spiritual traditions), feelings of joy and contentment are internal. They come from an acceptance of "What Is." They are not determined by waiting for a future occurrence or a change in past occurrences.

When you find yourself feeling stuck and unhappy, that can be symptoms of struggling. Usually, we are struggling with "What Is." When I was a chaplain, many patients in terminal conditions taught me a valuable lesson: Struggle ends in the acceptance of "What Is" and joy begins in a choice of how to move forward.

SPECIAL NOTE: When I have discussed this with some people, they have responded with "that seems so hopeless." In other words, some people confuse "Accept What Is" with "There Is No Hope." So, to clarify, there is no connection between hope and acceptance. Hope looks at what might happen, toward the positive in the future. Acceptance is about what has happened right up to this present moment. There is no changing "What Is." "What Might Be" has yet to be played out.

At the same time, knowing and accepting "What Is" often makes our hope a bit more realistic. What is possible to happen is different than what is probable to happen. And what is probable is often tied to where we are at this moment—not where we wish we were, but where we are.

CHAPTER 11

Control What You Can and Release the Rest

S ome days, it can seem like the world is spinning around us, just out of reach of our control. People make decisions that impact us—and yet we have no control over their actions. World events surround us but are just beyond our grasp (or even our touch).

And yet, most of us still *try* to jump in and control.

Interestingly, we often seem to attempt to control the things we cannot control, while simultaneously failing to control the things we can control. We choose the targets that guarantee frustration and failure. And we refuse the targets that might actually make a shift in our own lives.

You may notice that this particular Immutable Law is tied into the prior. We try to control what we won't accept. When we refuse to accept "What Is," we will try to control it in an attempt to get to "What We Want." Yet, those efforts are generally aimed at the wrong things.

More than that, we humans are very skilled at subtle forms of control.

Take, for example, worry. Many people give in to worry. Generally, worrying is just repeatedly building scenarios of what *might* happen. We usually worry about people for whom we care. And there is often a built-in belief, just below the surface, that by worrying, we can keep a bad thing from happening. It is a subtle attempt to control the world, and it is a confusion of care and concern. Many people believe that by worrying, they are caring and showing concern. But those worries? They are generally about things over which we have zero control.

Denial is another subtle form of control. If you refuse to acknowledge and accept that something has happened, it is your way of trying to control what is going on. You are pretending to have control of those events in your hands. Just last week, I had a client tell me, "I can't accept _____." She described an event that was beyond debate. It HAD happened. But since she did not want it to have happened, my client decided to actively refuse the event. She simply wanted to control an event that was beyond her control.

Similarly, when we are stuck in reaction mode, we are often trying to control something that is generally beyond our control. We can respond to events—accepting where we are and choosing our next path—but reacting to them is fighting against and pushing against that event in an attempt to keep it from happening (or having happened). Our reactivity is based on an effort to control.

This is particularly true when we make demands on others. When we try to make someone do something—usually something they do not want to do—we step into control. And even if you believe your reasons are for the best (and someone else may even objectively agree with you, that it is for the best), you are stepping into the role of trying to control things you cannot control. This often happens when something important to us is at risk.

Throughout my career, I have had the chance to help many people save their marriage. I have had an opportunity to watch repeated marital dynamics, and control is one of them. Whenever one spouse tries to control the other, it nearly always ends poorly. The one feeling controlled either abdicates responsibility or rebels against the one trying to control. Neither dynamic leads to healthy relating. Often, both end up miserable and angry. Sometimes, the struggle escalates to the point of putting the marriage at risk. And even at that moment, the temptation is to try to control the other person through reasoning, begging, pleading, and manipulating in an attempt to hold on and keep them in the marriage. It is often ineffective, based solely on the desire to control.

Parents often fall into this trap. From the moment a child is born, most parents want the best for their children. Parents want their children to be safe and to become successful adults. In the very beginning, parents can control the environment (to some degree) in order to keep their children safe. But at every stage of a child's life, a parent has less and less capacity to control things. (And really, it was an illusion of control from day one; as a child grows, the number of things a parent can control quickly dwindles.) Parents tend not to notice this as it is happening, continually trying to control things long after it is possible. If you've ever had a child who did not act the way you wanted, either in your presence or away from you, the child has already proven this point. Still, we parents give control a try!

How We Disobey This Law

Control is sneaky. We often try to control things for good and bad reasons. We often rationalize the "bad" reasons to see them as good. In the end, we usually think we are doing what we do (controlling) to help. The problem is, we often work to control things beyond our control.

For example, we have no control over other people's thoughts, beliefs, actions, or attitude. Yet we try to control them. Whenever we try to change someone's thinking (particularly when unsolicited), we are working on something over which we have no control. A person can think what that person wants to think. The same with beliefs. We all get to choose our beliefs. In fact, when we try to control what someone is thinking and believing, they generally dig into their thoughts and beliefs even deeper.

(Let me note that *control* and *influence* are very different. You may have the capacity to greatly influence those around you. Both consciously and unconsciously, we all influence those around us, and vice versa. Your parents' thoughts and beliefs likely influenced your perceptions about the world, shaping your beliefs and thoughts. The same is true for you and your children. And spouses constantly influence each other's thoughts. In fact, I am hoping that my writing will influence your thinking. The difference is often in the presentation. Influence happens in the midst of interactions over time. Attempts to control are often in reaction to something happening. A child might state a thought or belief you don't like, so you attempt to change it. That is when we disobey this law.)

Remember that thoughts and beliefs are internal. Each person can continue to think and believe what they want, regardless of external influence. Some people, feeling heavy control from another person, might state the "correct" thought or belief, yet hold to their own. And some may state the opposite, to prove a point—while their internal thoughts and beliefs remain different than stated.

This similarly applies to other people's actions. Other people will often choose actions over which we do not approve. And yet, we don't have the capacity to choose their actions. Children prove this point to their parents on an ongoing basis! Spouses often prove this point, acting in ways their spouse would not want. The simple truth is, without power or authority, we do not have control over actions. Even with power or authority, the control over actions is still often after-the-fact. We might penalize someone for their actions after they have taken action—thus, we didn't control the action, but we might be trying to control future actions (although, even this is doubtful).

It's not just other people we can't control. We also don't have control over the laws of physics. This is a painful realization (literally and figuratively). I witnessed this over and over as a chaplain in the hospital. Accidents follow the laws of physics. Momentum and inertia explained the "why" of many injuries. We cannot control those laws. When the laws of physics exert themselves upon us, we *want* to control them, but we can't. If I am running at full speed down a trail (this has happened multiple times), and trip on a root, the laws of physics will determine how that scenario ends. Usually, the law hurts. Still, we have no control over those laws.

Nor can we control biology. Aging happens. Illness happens. Biology marches forward. Eventually, you and I (and everyone around us) will die. Biology keeps moving toward that conclusion. As much as we want to stop this, biology is beyond our control. Yes, doctors can help deal with some biological issues (short-term), but they can't stop the underlying biology. Yes, we can take care of our bodies, stay in shape, eat healthily, and try to minimize risk. And yet, we will still die. We can pad our children, give them their shots, feed them well, and they can still get hurt or sick.

The fact is, we cannot control physics or biology. We want to, but we can't.

We also can't completely control our thoughts and fears. Related to the Law stating Thoughts Are Thoughts, our mind is designed to create thoughts. Many times, those thoughts lead to fears. We can't stop it from happening. Our mind thinks; we fear. The mind is going to do that—create thoughts— it's just what it does. And fears come from those thoughts. You *can* choose whether you keep hanging onto a thought that appears and allow fear to grow. But you can't control a thought popping into your mind; nor can you control the immediate fear that results. (Again, you still have a choice in what you do with those thoughts and fears.)

You also do not have control, obviously, over world events. And yet, some people keep a close eye on the news, as if those world events are in their control. For the vast majority of us, we have the capacity to make an impact in our own immediate sphere (we will get to that later), but have little capacity to impact the larger world stage. Even if you happen to be one of those bigger players (politicians, leaders in worldwide businesses or not-for-profits), you still have limited capacity in your bigger sphere.

We all have the responsibility to do what we can to make the world a better place, to fight injustice, and to care for those on the margins. We all have the responsibility to care for the environment and leave the world just a little better than we found it. What I notice, though, is the energy people expend worrying about events over which they have no control. People glue themselves to the "news" to "stay informed" and "be active." Yet those events continue to unravel. And the "news" has one purpose: to keep your eyeballs on the screen and your ears engaged, for the benefit of advertisers. Stories are chosen and produced to keep you tuned.

Be informed and take action where you can, but don't confuse that mass of information as describing anything you can actually control.

How We Obey This Law

This law is about controlling what you can and releasing the rest. So, let's start with what you *can* control. What *can* you control?

1) Remember the 3 A's: Aspirations, Attitudes, and Actions. We all have the capacity to control our aspirations, attitudes, and actions.

While we can't control the thoughts that pop into our head, nor the fears those thoughts trigger, we do have control over our aspirations—our hopes and dreams, the desired direction of our life.

Aspirations are not quite the opposite of fears. They are interlinked. For every major fear you have, there is a corresponding aspiration. For every dream or aspiration you have, there is a corresponding fear. Your aspirations are about what you want to be and accomplish in life.

We get to choose what we pursue and the paths to get there. We get to move toward our purpose. Fears and aspirations both tend to have a future tense to them. Fears will arise (and, as we previously discussed, *can* be pointing you toward important things); aspirations are chosen. And since we choose them, we control them. Controlling your aspirations is different than controlling your destiny. You can choose where you want to go, but not necessarily if you will get there.

When I work with people trying to save their marriage, there is an aspiration to have a great marriage. Usually, there is an aspiration to improve both themselves and the relationship. Each person coming into my program can choose (and usually has already chosen) that aspiration. But that does not guarantee success. A spouse, at least in most parts of the world, can still refuse to remain in the marriage. A spouse can still choose to break the boundaries of marriage, betraying their partner and choosing another person.

A person can also choose his or her attitude. (This is not the same as when your parent said, "I don't like your attitude." That usually meant your actions and emotional response were not what your parents wanted—since it was a challenge to them!)

Ray is the person who taught me to Scuba dive. He also helped me through the process of becoming an instructor. He and I then taught together for a few years. Ray is an exceptional person who has always been clear about attitude. In the first Scuba class, Ray requests that students maintain a "PMA," a Positive Mental Attitude. Ray does not request that everyone be happy and smiling, but that each person is willing to try and learn. PMA means that instead of saying, at the beginning of an exercise, "I can't do that," to say, "I will try that." Attitude is an alignment with capacity. "I can do that," "I will do that," "I will figure this out," or "I will try that," is an attitude you can choose. You can default to "I can't do that," "I won't do that," or "I won't even try that," but you can *choose* to move the other way. We all get to control and choose our attitude.

We also control our actions—what we *do*. Like it or not, we have control over whether we hurt or help. We control how we move in the world. This is a tough one because we all do things we later regret (or at least feel bad about). We like to pretend we *can't* control our actions, but we do. There are always situations—perhaps with someone in authority—where we would not have acted that way. Yelled at a friend? You likely wouldn't yell at a police officer. Threw an object in anger? You probably would not throw that object while standing in a courtroom. If you can choose an action in one place, it is a fair bet that you can choose it in any place.

The real question—when it comes to aspirations, attitudes, or actions—is whether or not we *choose* to control them. This is where we notice the interplay between the laws. When we decide to choose our aspirations, attitude, and actions, we are choosing to obey the Law of Responsibility.

2) Set boundaries and raise standards. We also have control over two ways we interact with the world. We can control our boundaries and our standards. Boundaries are what you will allow (and not allow) others to do toward you. It is, in essence, your "No" to others' behavior. Can others yell at you, call you names, take advantage of you, and many other behaviors? Or do you stop them? These are your boundaries. We get to choose our boundaries. (If you want to understand boundaries and how to set them, listen to my podcast on boundaries: http://thriveology.com/boundary)

Standards are what you expect of yourself. It is your "Yes" to the world on how you will "Show Up." "Yes, I will be honest." "Yes, I will be loving." "Yes, I will show respect." There are a myriad of standards you might hold for yourself. To be clear: we all have standards, whether we are aware of them or not. The question is whether we are noticing and choosing, and then raising our standards. If not, they tend to be weak and inconsistent. (If you want to understand standards and how to raise them, listen to my podcast on standards: http://thriveology.com/standard).

The point is, we get to choose how we allow others to treat us, and how we will treat others. We choose our No's and Yes's in interacting with the world. But only when we notice we can, and when we decide to choose.

3) Release the rest. There is another part to this law: Release the Rest. If we can't control it, we need to release it—to stop trying to control it. The first step is to recognize what you can and can't change. If you find it falls within your aspirations, attitude, actions, boundaries, or standards, decide what you want to do and take responsibility for doing it. If you can't control it (areas outside the above—including other people's aspirations, attitudes, and actions), release it.

Do notice a point of overlap: someone else's actions may violate your boundaries. You can choose to stop their action toward you, but not how they act in the world. In other words, you can decide you will not allow someone to yell at you, but you can't decide they will not yell at anyone. Just at you. (You may need to protect those who cannot protect themselves, such as small children. But even then, your task is to protect the person receiving the action, not change the person acting.)

There is also a subtle way we like to play at control: worry. Worry is really fear. It is usually about things you cannot control or do anything about. We often worry as a substitute for acting. If we can act, we should act. If we can't, worrying is just a waste of energy. It often becomes a habit. Many times, people believe the thought causing the worry is real or is important. Generally, when we can't do anything about it, we are better served by working to let go of the worry than continuing to worry. Remember, we can't control fears that pop into our minds. But we do get to choose whether we continue to dwell on those fears or whether we let them dissipate.

Here are three steps to help you release what you can't control:

1) Use Belly Breathing. This technique we previously discussed will help you move through anxious moments. Just because we can recognize what we can't control, it does not mean the worry instantly evaporates. When it comes, Belly Breathe through it. The worry will dissipate from lack of attention.

2) Build Discernment. Get better and better at identifying the difference between what you can control and what you can't control. We all have "habits of mind" that we have developed over a lifetime. One habit is trying to control what we can't and failing to control what we can. The "discernment muscle" is a bit weak in many people, but, with practice, it grows stronger. You'll become more and more clear on what you can control (and then choose to control) and what you can't (and then choose to release).

3) Build Appreciation/Gratitude. We often build a deep "fear rut" in our mind. The more we allow fear to dominate and choose our behavior, the more it takes hold. Anything that comes into the mind tends to get caught in that "fear rut." We just naturally go there—straight into fear. We can choose to be appreciative and to express gratitude. We can choose to focus on what we appreciate in life. When we focus on what we appreciate, our brain shifts from fear to love. We build an "appreciation rut" where we default to our aspirational side. Fear will appear, but aspiration will take over.

Choose your aspirations, attitude, and actions. Set your boundaries. Raise your standards. That is what you CAN control. Choose to control it. Release the rest.

CHAPTER 12

Forgive to Fully Live

When something (or someone) hurts us, we hold onto it. That makes some sense from a survival perspective where you are well-served to remember circumstances that are dangerous. Except we choose to take it a step further. We choose to become a victim of the scenario (a choice we don't necessarily know we are making), and that keeps us stuck.

There is a difference between believing that the shadow on the grass behind that rock on the savanna is a dangerous predator—since it was a predator the last time you saw it—and believing that the friend who said something bad about you and/or your family is a threat to your well-being. The same wiring in the brain plays into both. The question is only in how we hold onto the event.

Holding on to the event is refusing to forgive.

Let's say you are walking along a path, with a cliff rising to your left. As you move beside the cliff, someone above you dislodges a sharp rock. Perhaps it was on purpose, but maybe it was accidental. From your perspective, you can't tell the difference. The rock tumbles down and strikes your shoulder, cutting and hurting you, then lands at your feet.

You reach down, angrily, and snatch up the rock. You hold it tightly, shaking your fist in the air toward the top of the hill, saying, "I'm not going to forget this!" The rock cuts into your tightly fisted hand injuring you a second time as you grip it. In the meantime, the other person has continued on their way, either unaware or uncaring of the injury.

Refusing to let go of that rock leads to continual injury of the person gripping the rock; it does little to the one who dislodged it in the first place.

Letting go of the rock is really what forgiveness is about.

Much of my work over the years has been with people in the aftermath of some event. Perhaps it was poor parenting, or maybe their parents were abusive. Perhaps it was a traumatic event, or maybe it was lots of smaller but hurtful events along the way. In the aftermath, my clients have struggled with letting go of the event. For some, that event becomes their identity; life becomes organized around that event.

Tightly gripping the event continues to hurt the person holding on. And yet, we humans seem to have the unique capability of holding tightly to our hurts, causing continued harm to ourselves. (Let me be clear: I also work to release my own hurts, just like every other person. This law is about practice, not perfection.)

Hurts from the past hold us hostage until we shift to forgiving. Lewis Smedes writes, "To forgive is to set a prisoner free and to discover that the prisoner was you." We hold onto the hurts to make a point, a reminder, a statement—and we end up re-injured.

The problem is, the idea of "forgive" is full of extra meanings and myths. It has become a religious admonition of "have to," versus the spiritual truth of "get to." You don't "have to" forgive. You "get to" forgive so you can release and move forward.

Words are interesting. They can sometimes point to inner meaning. The word "forgive" shares a Latin root with *perdonare,* before passing through Germanic, into English. That word, *perdonare,* meant "to forgive completely, without reservation," in Latin. And it is closely related to the word, "pardon." When someone is pardoned, they are released from the offense. The Aramaic (and a closely related Hebrew) word *shbag,* used to indicate forgiveness, means "to untie." Both words give us some guidance. We forgive completely so that we are untied from that event.

In the abstract, most of us agree that forgiving is an important thing—especially if we are the ones wanting to be forgiven. Forgiving something painful and important, though, is a bit less abstract. It becomes real when pointed toward something difficult. It is more daunting when it is personal.

An interesting thing happens when I am teaching on forgiveness. It's a brain "hiccup" that seems to happen consistently. In the beginning, I discuss the fact that forgiving is for the person doing the forgiving—it unties them from the event and/or person so that they can move forward. Forgiving is *FOR* the forgiver. It is the release from the hurt. We carefully work through this information and participants agree with me (in the abstract, as a concept).

I then ask, "What are some 'unforgiveables' that someone might do? What could someone do that someone should just *not* forgive?"

The trap is set.

And every time it is also sprung.

Participants will begin to name horrid events that should not be forgiven. Horrible action after terrible action is noted.

Then I return to the prior information: Forgiving is *FOR* the forgiver. Not the offender.

Which means I have to remind them of one important thing about forgiveness: Forgiving does NOT equal forgetting. It does NOT remove penalties. It does NOT free the offender.

It frees the forgiver.

Why, then, if we know this in the abstract, do we immediately return to the "unforgiveables"? Because we carry around a mess in our minds about forgiving.

Forgiving Is NOT Forgetting

We can forgive someone and still remember that we were hurt. In fact, if you forget, forgiving is irrelevant. The event goes away, anyway.

Forgiveness is about understanding the other person differently. It is understanding events differently. It is *not* pretending something didn't happen. It is understanding it from a different perspective.

I've noted that a major part of my career has been to work with troubled marriages. A frequent issue in troubled marriages is infidelity. Along with the discovered affair comes tremendous pain. In fact, infidelity often makes that list of "unforgiveables."

In my experience, there are two roots of infidelity. One root reason is addiction. Someone is either addicted to sex or relationships, leading to infidelity as a way of getting their "fix." The other root reason is about disconnection. When a marriage is disconnected, and someone does not maintain appropriate boundaries, an affair can happen.

The person who suffers the affair can take it personally—that the spouse "meant" to hurt him or her by having an affair. Or that spouse can see the cheating from another perspective. It may be addiction—which changes the perspective. It may be from disconnection—which also changes the perspective.

Let me be clear: the person who cheated is 100% responsible for their actions. There can still be consequences. The marriage may still end. But by not forgiving, the person who suffered the affair is trapped into the hurt of infidelity. The affair is taken personally; yes, their spouse cheated *against* them, but they miss their spouse's motivation of doing it *for* him/herself.

People generally act *for* themselves, versus *against* someone else.

In fact, that one truth is the beginning point of forgiving. It makes the event about the offender, not the injured. Let me say it again: People primarily do things FOR themselves, not AGAINST others.

Measure that against yourself. Think back to a time when you caused injury of some sort, emotional or otherwise, to someone. Was your motivation for yourself? Were you protecting yourself in some way? Perhaps you did not want to be embarrassed. Perhaps you wanted to look stronger than you felt. Perhaps you were defending against some perceived threat. I would bet your primary motivation was FOR you. It may have hurt another person, but that was not your primary intention.

We all suffer from what social scientists call the "attribution error:" If *you* do something wrong, I tend to attribute it to a character flaw. But if *I* do something wrong (even the same thing), I will tend to view it as a mistake. In other words, people tend to let themselves off the hook for doing the exact same thing they hold against someone else.

Which is right? Mistake or flaw? Probably some of both. The problem is we hold onto what others do and forget what we do. Forgiving is really seeing things with more **clarity** and **empathy**.

Clarity comes from seeing the actions from a fair perspective. Have you ever had the experience where someone is describing a "very bad" event that happened to them and all the while you are wondering what the fuss is about? Or perhaps you have been telling someone about an event that happened to you and notice the listener seems to be missing the severity of what happened? Usually, that means there is some clarity lacking from your perspective. We do tend to *catastrophize* events, making them bigger.

Empathy comes from understanding where the other person is coming from. Perhaps their angry action was not so much anger with you as being angry about something else and reacting with you. Perhaps their reaction was not just about you but based on other life events for them. It may have come from their own place of pain (in fact, it *likely* did).

Clarity gives a realistic perspective. Empathy adds an understanding perspective.

To be clear, people do bad things; there are bad people. To reiterate, this also does not mean there are no consequences. It means you are not going to let a hurtful action continue to harm you by holding onto it. This is about minimizing damage, not pretending it didn't happen.

I try to start with a general perspective that I do not see things as clearly as I could. I try to assume that and then look for proof. And I don't always have to figure out *what* is going on with someone (empathy) to assume that *something* is going on. This empathy perspective just assumes that others are having struggles like I am and may not be acting from their better selves.

For the most part, forgiving is a response to something that has already happened. The event is most often in either the immediate past or long ago.

Something has happened. It hurt. The question is what happens next. Forgiving is not about forgetting, nor is it about the event having no consequences. But it might be about remembering differently.

I've noticed a trend with marital problems. Over and over, one person will tell me about the "horrible actions" of their spouse. Their spouse agrees the event happened but then tells me about the context—often including something the offended spouse did prior to the offense. The story then goes one layer deeper; the first spouse replies, "Yeah, but..." and adds another action, another layer, another wrinkle, from the other spouse. This little game goes on for some time. I do believe that if I let it play out, we would eventually be hearing stories from before either was even born!

Sometimes, remembering events requires a different context. Sometimes, it is about remembering with empathy for the other person. Sometimes, it is about remembering with an eye to one's own culpability in the process. Always, it is choosing to move toward forgiveness.

Remember, forgiving releases the forgiver, regardless of the forgiven.

How We Disobey This Law

This law, Forgive to Live, is disobeyed by one simple thing: not forgiving. When we refuse to forgive, we become hostage to the actions of another person. It affects our mood, thoughts, and actions. It robs us of energy and potential. Since humans are really designed to find purpose, create meaning, and make an impact (we will discuss this later), when energy is lost, we can miss out on our design. Simply put, we miss out on purpose, meaning, and impact.

People disobey this Immutable Law because forgiving is misunderstood. People disobey this law because they believe it will protect them to hold on. People disobey this law because it maintains a "life story" of not taking responsibility and of being the victim. And in the process, people are robbed of living fully, of thriving.

How We Obey This Law

The first step in obeying this law is simply working to understand forgiveness—free from the myths and misunderstandings that keep us away from forgiving. It is to understand that forgiving is not about forgetting. Painful life events do not need to be forgotten. Pain dissipates when we release ourselves from the event, not by pretending the event didn't happen.

It is about understanding that someone can be forgiven and still held to consequences for their behavior. If someone hurts me, I can choose whether to be in a relationship with them, regardless of forgiving that person. I can forgive and decide to not be in a relationship, or I can forgive and establish a new relationship.

We also obey this law when we commit to forgiving. Do notice that committing to forgiving is not the same as having forgiven. Forgiveness is a process. It does not happen overnight. A decision to forgive is the first step. After that, it takes some work. We obey this law as soon as we head in the direction of forgiving. It happens when we commit to forgiving.

(If you need more help with the process of forgiving, here is a resource to help: http://thriveology.com/forgive)

CHAPTER 13

Life Is In the NOW

Groucho Marx said, "I, not events, have the power to make me happy or unhappy today. I can choose which it shall be. Yesterday is dead, tomorrow hasn't arrived yet. I have just one day, today, and I'm going to be happy in it."

Some days, I envy my dog. He seems to have "now" down pat. If he is tired, he naps. If there is a sunbeam, he finds it and enjoys it. He is excited to do something. But he seems equally content to hang out.

In the warmer days, I make a habit of getting 15 to 20 minutes of sunlight, with as minimal clothing as acceptable by the neighborhood and the weather. I recline on my deck and close my eyes to take in the warm sunshine. My dog, Ziggy, curls up beside me. Often, he is breathing quietly, almost instantly napping. I am trying to chase thoughts of what needs to be done out of my mind. I have to work at it. He lives the now.

Humans have a natural time orientation that seems mostly unique to humans. Sure, by instinct, animals gather resources for the coming seasons. Sure, by instinct, animals recall places where something dangerous happened. But that is a bit different than a human choosing to think about a time, past or future, by choice.

Do you remember holidays when you were a child? Can you recall Christmases or birthdays of your childhood? Notice how you immediately start recalling moments, have flashes of memories. And if you spent some time doing this, you might be able to rebuild many events of those days, simply because you have a reference point to pull from.

Or I could ask you about upcoming plans for vacation. If you have any, you can start telling me about the dates and plans. You are purposely choosing to think forward in your imagination.

This uniquely human ability can also be a curse. Many times, people spend their time thinking about other times. They get caught up in re-living the past or pre-living the future. Interestingly, much of the time spent in the past or future is not about the good moments but the tough moments. And even if it was spent on the good moments, it is not spent on the moments of now.

Several years back, I was leading a class on clearing out our mental clutter. We were discussing thoughts and the mind—really, we were discussing how our thoughts can often lead us into distress. Someone asked me about depression and anxiety. I noted that when people get stuck in past painful thoughts, they tend to get depressed. I also noted that when people get caught in fearful future thoughts, they experience anxiety. Past thoughts lead to depression and future thoughts lead to anxiety. Brilliant, I thought. But I am not the first to think that. The same idea has been attributed to Lao Tzu. Whether that is accurate or not, I am clearly not the first to stumble upon it.

Yes, it is possible to remember things that happened and not become depressed. Yes, it is possible to plan for the future and not become anxious. And it is possible to be stuck in the past or future with depression or anxiety.

It is more likely that all of us give up moments of living for moments lived and moments that might be lived. How many times have you been doing one thing while focused on another? Perhaps you are spending time with the kids at a park, but you are focused on what you need to do at work or home. Then you go to work or start a home project, only to find yourself focused on the need to spend time with the kids. Wherever you are, your mind is somewhere else—in another time or another place.

I admit that I am not good at remembering to take a photo during an event. Partly, it just isn't my mindset. But partly, I notice that when people are taking photos and videos, they are often removed from the actual event. They are no longer participants of the moment, but participants in the video or photo. They are removed observers; instead of experiencing the event, they are focused on the camera. I recognize that for many people, this is their hobby—where they want to focus. But it creates a useful analogy of what we do with our thoughts. We remove ourselves from the moment—lost in thoughts about the past, thoughts about that moment, or thoughts about the future. The experience is lost to thoughts. We become removed from the moment.

Let me be clear: many people have wonderful memories from the past. And many people have great plans for the future. Nothing is wrong with memories and plans. But many people focus on the painful memories of the past, dragging the pain into the moment. Others become so anxious over the future that they pull the anxiety into the present. More than that, many people lose the present moment with a layer of thoughts, memories, and worries.

How We Disobey This Law

Life is in the now. That's the law. So, when we constantly go toward past/future orientations, we lose the moment. The moment, ironically, is what builds those memories and builds toward the future.

The real hang-up about the past? It is a desire to "redo" it. In other words, often, a focus on the past is really a desire to either have it happen differently than it did or re-live it again. In a prior chapter, we discussed "Reverse Fatalism," the need to accept what happened as having happened. The need to accept "What Is," which is a result of the past. Sometimes, people stay stuck in the past, trying to find a way to redo it. Others simply want to return to the past because it offers something that feels safer than current life.

The real problem with the future? It can keep us scanning for "what's next," either as a place of fear or as an escape from now. And in the process, we miss NOW. Have you ever been talking with someone at a party, knowing they were looking beyond you for the next person to see? You were just in the way of whatever was next. And likely, so was the next person. When people live for "what's next," what's Now gets little focus. And in the process, not much comes from Now.

How We Obey This Law

1) Start the day with the clarity of living in the moment. It won't last the entire day, but that's okay. You will drift into your thoughts throughout the day. You will be tempted to be pulled into the past, the future, and away from the present—all through the day. You will have times of being distracted away from the present moment. That's just the way our mind works.

But if you start each day with the intention of being present, in the moment, you will spend more moments in the present. Notice something interesting: if you find you are in the present moment, really present, you might start telling yourself, "Hey, I'm present. I'm in the moment." And that present moment is lost to thinking.

Which leads us to a practice going back centuries, both in Eastern and Western culture.

2) Practice mindfulness. Being mindful is merely focusing on what is happening right now. It is not so much thinking about the present, but being in the present, both in times of calm and times of stress. Remember that metaphor of photography? That moment when you step back away from the present, you stop being present.

An easy way to practice mindfulness is to purposefully envelope yourself in the experience. If you are at the park, allow your senses to take in your surroundings. Notice how it feels on your feet as you walk. Notice the smells around you. Notice the sounds and noises. Can you taste the air? In other words, immerse yourself in the sensual experience of the park. The more we surround ourselves in the sensual, the less lost in our thoughts we become. Our senses take in the present (sight, smell, sound, taste, and touch).

You can do the same with a meal. Or even a piece of fruit. As I write this, we have a fruit bowl on the kitchen island. It has been there the entire time, and I have failed to notice the colors of each fruit, (the specks of discoloration, too). I can smell the mandarins in the bowl; I can smell the ripening banana. When I spend just a bit of time, my senses take in the smells. And, if I were so inclined, I could sit and taste the fruit—fully aware of the experience.

I've noticed that many times, we do the exact opposite of that experience. I was walking through a beautiful park the other day. Several parents were there with their kids. Each parent was engrossed with their smartphones. They were not experiencing the park.

I walked a bit further. It was around lunchtime, so some people were eating. They were sitting in a beautiful park, eating what should be tasty food, and yet they were lost in a mobile device. To be clear, they were neither fully present to the park nor to lunch nor even to their phone. They were lost between all those worlds, and in the process, no longer in the present.

Mindfulness is simply turning your attention to what you are doing. It is experiencing the experience. Practicing that—focusing the senses on the experience—brings us back to the present. (For more help with mindfulness, here is some further explanation: http://thriveology.com/mindfulness)

3) Practice presence. When you are with someone else, be present. Focus on the words you are hearing (and the emotions behind them) rather than pondering your next response. Use the conversation as an interaction. Many people interact as merely an interruption to their own ideas being spoken, leading to people talking AT each other, not WITH each other.

Let the interaction be about learning and widening perspective. And resist the urge to control the conversation, the other person, or the other person's beliefs and opinions.

CHAPTER 14

Time Is Our Most Precious Commodity

66 "Time is money," he said. And off he rushed to work.

He was a client of mine. Hard-working, determined, talented. "Bob" was a litigation attorney—and he won his cases. Lots. So, he had many people waiting at his door for advice.

Not being happy with his life, Bob found his way to my office, where he would fuss and complain about all the people needing his help. Bob confessed he didn't like what he was doing anymore. In fact, he dreaded it every day. The alarm went off at five in the morning. He was at his desk by 6:30. Most days, he left the office at 7:30 that night, files in hand to work on after dinner. Days in court or preparing for court led Bob to feel stressed and exhausted. But every day, he climbed back on the wheel and went round and round.

Except for a few hours here and there. One was in my office, as Bob tried to figure out how to make life worthwhile. We spoke about meaning and purpose. We talked about making a difference. Then off Bob would go, usually right back to court. In fact, many sessions were scheduled last-minute—or canceled—thanks to fickle court timing and settlements.

At the end of our session, Bob would jump off my couch, grab his suit coat and hit the door saying, "Time is money," as he slid out of my office.

An hour of Bob's time cost six times the cost of an hour of mine. And Bob's schedule was full. Bob, by any measure, had quite a lucrative lifestyle.

But not much of a life.

Then, Bob began to struggle with his schedule. He just didn't feel well. The food he shoveled in was not sitting well. This was always the case since Bob really didn't care what he shoved in—which did lead to indigestion by evening. But now, Bob was in a constant state of discomfort. When he went to bed, it was worse.

I noticed Bob's coloring was off. He blamed it on an unusually long case. "I'll check on it when the case is over," he told me.

Bob's wife was concerned. He was moving slower, was not feeling well, and was beginning to not look well.

Finally, Bob relented, "If it will make you happy," he said to his wife and me.

The doctor immediately hospitalized Bob. Tests revealed pancreatic cancer. Stage four.

Treatment left Bob's body ravaged. Six months later, Bob died.

I thought back to those parting words from Bob. He said it to rib me. The first time he said it was at the beginning of our first session. He said, "I'm not happy. My wife is tired of it; so, here I am. Let's figure this out, but let's not waste time. Time is money."

"Bob," I responded the first time, "that is an absolute lie. Time is NOT money. Money is money and time is time." Bob responded by saying that same line at the end of every single session. With a smile. As he rushed out the door.

In one of our last meetings, Bob said, "I regret that. I said it to my wife, my children, and myself. For years. You challenged me. But people paid me a lot for my time. I knew what you meant, but I liked how much I could charge for my time. I traded my life for money. What do I have? Stuff."

A month later, Bob was dead.

Let me be clear: It is entirely possible that if Bob had gone at a slower pace, or worked a different job, or took days off, he would still be dead at way too young an age from pancreatic cancer. One major fact is that none of us are going to get out of this life alive.

The question is not about Bob trading his health for money. That is entirely possible. But we have no way of knowing. I do know this: Bob was not enjoying life while he was living it.

At one point, early in his illness, Bob asked, "Why did you always roll your eyes when I said, 'Time is money'? It just seems to me that is the truth for most people. Hourly employees trade hours for a paycheck. My professional friends do it, too. Billable hours are the currency of my attorney, doctor, accountant, and … well, therapist. Just seems that is true."

"Bob," I responded, "that hour is certainly the measurement of pay. But here is the thing: Money is a commodity that is elastic and replaceable. Time is a commodity that once you spend it, it is gone forever. If I lose money, I can make more. I can spend less. It is a resource that can grow. Time is diminishing. Once I spend it, it is gone. I can't buy it back."

Each of us has a life to spend. We don't know how long it might be. Yet each day, we have to decide how to spend the time of that day. The day will pass, no matter what. We will arrive at the end of the day, that time forever gone.

And yet many times, we spend that time without regard to the preciousness of the resource.

Let me be clear: This is not a "don't waste time" perspective. It is more about recognizing and being conscious of how the time is being spent. It is deciding whether you are spending your time the way you want, not whether you are spending time. That happens regardless.

While I am not perfect at this, I am much more aware of my time these days. In fact, I call this part of my life "Bonus Time." I didn't actually think I would have it.

Over a decade ago, I got sick. It took about six weeks for the doctors to figure it out. During that time, I dragged myself to the office and saw clients. Then I dragged myself home and slept. My day started with maxing out on over-the-counter painkillers. But I was always hurting.

Then, one day in the doctor's office, I showed the doctor some rashes that had developed on my legs (my badly swollen feet already overflowed my shoes). He was alarmed. After an x-ray and being poked at by another doctor, my doc shared his suspicion about my illness. He told me it was bad. But he wanted confirmation.

To be honest, much of that time was spent in a haze of feeling bad and being exhausted. We got confirmation. The haze was cut like a laser when I heard the doctor tell my wife there was an 86% chance of total disability, followed by death.

From there, I had the "opportunity" to visit a number of specialists. The goal was not so much to cure me. It was to assess the damage already done. Still miserable, I dragged myself from specialist to specialist. All told me I hadn't suffered damage yet, but also told me what to expect. It was not a pretty picture.

Along the way, the doctor who was to manage my illness and eventual decline announced my reprieve. He told me that while I was miserable, I was fortunate. Generally, the illness I had was chronic, continually damaging to a body, and a slowly deteriorating disease. As it turns out, there is a rare acute version of my particular rare illness. The downside was that the "acute" meant "feel awful." The upside was I would recover. And as you may have surmised, I did recover.

Bonus time.

As I said, I got a reprieve. It will likely not be that illness I will die from. That illness burned out and is pretty much a non-issue for me. But something will, at some point, lead to my death.

Time changes when you think there is not going to be more. I contemplated the fact that I might not be able to enjoy time with my family, go on vacation, contribute to society (and my family). I realized I could have lost opportunities to live without any warning.

And there was no turning back. We truly never know when we do the "last time" of anything. Which leads to treasuring "each time."

And that leads us back to "time."

It is the one commodity you cannot replace. Lose money? Make more. Lose friends and relationships? A few billion people are out there. Lose a house? There are others, even in your neighborhood. Lose a job? Yep, there are others.

Time, as it passes, is gone. Irreplaceable. Non-extendable.

And yet we treat it with little regard.

How We Disobey This Law

When we treat time as a common commodity—or even fail to treat it as a commodity—we disobey this law.

And when we spend time on things that don't really matter—don't bring us purpose, joy, or passion, or don't make a difference in the world—we disobey this law.

How We Obey This Law

Let me be clear: I am **not** advocating that every moment of every day needs to be filled with activity. I am not suggesting rest and recreation are worthless. Human life is more like breathing. There are times to breathe in and times to breathe out. Times to act and times to rest. Times to move and times to be still.

I am more addressing an overall perspective on life. Are you involved in activities and actions that bring you meaning and purpose? Do you feel passionate about your involvement?

Every job, activity, and task can have mundane (even boring) parts. They are unavoidable. But they lead back to something bigger.

When we take scuba students on check out dives, I notice what happens. People love the dive. They are excited at the beginning, even if they struggle to get their gear together. And during the dive, I can see the rapture on their faces. The dive brings joy and excitement. Then, after the dive, it is time to clean the gear. Often, students would disappear during those times. Given their adult status, and the fact that at the end of the dive, they were certified and no longer under our guidance, we never forced anyone to help. But I am also clear that the mundane, boring, tiring job of cleaning the equipment *is part of* the dive. You have to clean the equipment so that you can enjoy a safe dive the next time.

Life is that way. I am not suggesting every minute is a mountain-top experience. Sometimes, you are preparing to climb. Sometimes, you are hiking up the tough terrain. Sometimes, you are hiking down after the view, soaking your feet, and resting. But those moments are all part of the mountain-top experience.

The problem is not the mundane parts of the meaningful; it is the lack of meaningful. Recharging is essential. In fact, if we don't take the time to recharge and recreate, any other action will be from exhaustion. The opportunity for meaning drops. And time is once again, squandered.

My concern is more about a lack of awareness on how time is being spent. When it is consciously spent, we acknowledge the precious commodity it is. When it just slips through our fingers, we devalue it.

Time, unlike money, cannot be saved. It is a commodity that must be spent. The question is, how will you spend it? It will pass either way.

Stephen Covey suggests we always "begin with the end in mind." In other words, whenever we start a project, we begin with what we want to happen and build toward that. This is one clear way of valuing time. Whenever you start a new venture, project, or experience, you can start with the question of what you want out of it.

Why does this change the commodity of time? You become clear of the benefit to spending the time. Will the "end result" justify the amount of time invested? Is it worth the spent time, given the outcome desired? (You may not get the desired outcome, just like a financial investment does not always come to fruition. But does it have the potential for a "return on investment" of time and energy?)

Many times, we discover, at the end of a project, that we spent our time and energy on something we didn't really care about. The investment is gone; the time has been paid—only to discover that there was no desired benefit at the end.

(Sometimes, you may decide that the desired end was "fun," entertainment, or just experience. But even then, you will have chosen to invest the time, rather than it simply slipping away.)

Be clear on how you "spend," "save," "waste," and "invest" your time. It is an ever-dwindling commodity in your life—and it is your choice on how you use the time you have to do what you want. It will pass. Choose what happens during that span. Your time is given to you. You have to spend it, use it up—even if you don't know exactly how much you have.

Make it well-spent. That time is precious. It is your most precious commodity.

CHAPTER 15

We Live In Fear or Love

S cientists are still working to explain the interplay between your thoughts, mind, and brain. As it turns out, thinking alters physiology. And brain physiology affects thinking. For example, we know that some people have much more active and exaggerated fear mechanisms in their brains. Many times, this is a result of living in a constant state of fear—and those active fear areas of the brain cause more fearful thoughts.

As we have discussed, you can't help what thoughts pop into your head. Your mind is designed to create all sorts of thoughts—some will help, some will hinder. But, as we have also discussed, you do have a choice in how you sort and hold onto any of these thoughts.

Those choices influence your brain structure. Every time you have a thought, there is a firing of brain synapse. If you consistently have that same thought over and over, it strengthens the connections of that "thought circuit." The same is true for actions you take: the more you take an action, the more reinforced that circuit in your brain becomes until it is automatic. We call that a "habit." And we create thought habits by the repeated thoughts we have.

This is a powerful tool—or a powerful trap. It all depends on how you use this fact. If you have and hold fearful thoughts, you create stronger fear circuits in your brain. If you have and hold more appreciative (or loving) thoughts, you create stronger appreciation circuits in your brain. And this causes you to have even more fearful—or appreciative and loving—thoughts.

Scientists have come to understand your brain exists on three distinct levels (this is known as the "triune brain theory"), due to biological development through the millennia. The part of the brain that is most primitive is the part of the brain existing to simply keep you alive. It is the "reptilian" brain, as poetically described by the scientists. This part of the brain is what we share with all creeping, crawling, swimming, and flying creatures (yep, even snakes and other reptiles). It keeps you safe and gets you into trouble on a regular basis.

The next level of the brain is the limbic or "mammalian" brain. We share it with warm-blooded creatures. Mammals tend to live in connection to others in their species. Some are loners, and others are pack creatures (this seems to be somewhat true with humans, too). But they still rely on each other.

Reptiles lay eggs and leave, or give birth and leave. No nurturing those babies. They are on their own, fending for themselves, and using instinct, which works pretty well. Mammals tend to need much more nurture and help. All the way up to humans, who tend to nurture their young ones for nearly two decades (or more!). Some mammals stay in a pack for their entire lives. Others split off. But they still have an affinity for each other.

The limbic system creates this affinity, this connection, through emotions; both emotions of connection and repulsion. We connect with "our own," even through repulsion from "others." Part of connection is done through defining who is and who is not part of the group. This is done by feelings of love and fear/hate.

Then, there is that top level of the brain, seemingly more developed in humans than other creatures. The neocortex gives us reasoning capacity and language. Language changes everything. While our memories are partly stored as images, we can recall them through language. Think (notice how you do this) about a party or gathering you might have attended where you reminisced. You or your friends may have started with "Remember that time..." Everybody turns to their file of memories and replays that one. The way it is remembered is very individual, but most will recall a particularly vivid event.

As far as we can tell, other creatures that communicate with each other don't spend much time reminiscing about the past or thinking about the future—that is, beyond the immediate hunt for food.

We humans have these three levels in our brain: reptilian, limbic, and neocortex. These levels of the brain are cobbled together in ways that are functional, even if not perfect. The system is optimized for survival, which makes sense. At a base level, if you don't survive, you can't move toward thriving. But that same wiring can also trap you in "survival mode."

Using the brain structure to thrive is more important than letting the structure rule your life in fear. The brain's fear is tied to survival in a world much more dangerous than the one you now occupy. And yet, the fear part of your brain likely hijacks your life on a daily basis.

And as the fear mechanism "fear-jacks" you, the fear wiring strengthens. When we live in fear, fear gets stronger. When we shift, we make a choice to thrive, and our thrive wiring strengthens.

Reptiles react to threats by either fighting or fleeing (fight/flight mode). There really isn't an emotion associated. Approach an alligator, and he is assessing his options. Are you a threat or a meal? Does he need to prepare for a fight, for a sprint, or for dinner? There is no real anger (or joy) in seeing you coming. Only threat assessment.

But mammals have a bit more of an emotional response. Have you ever seen an angry dog? Approach a dog, and there is the same threat assessment. But if you were the one who took his food or smacked him for no reason yesterday, there may also be an angry response. Or, there may be a wagging tail of affinity if you were the one who gave him a bone on the last visit. Emotions are attached to your approach. The limbic system is responsible for that added layer of emotion.

Humans can reason themselves right out of (or right into) a threat. Which means that humans are using language and reasoning to take the threat to a conversational level. Have you ever had a consistent angry response with someone, only to decide to change it? Perhaps you had a negative response with a co-worker. Every time you see that person, you have a strong, angry response. Then, you discover some humanizing fact. Perhaps they suffer from a disease that makes them moody. Or maybe they volunteer at a homeless shelter and had been up all night before they argued with you. Suddenly, that one extra fact shifts your thinking about that person. The person did not change, but your thinking about that person and the situation shifted. And your feelings shifted.

In reality, you also changed your brain phase. You went from fear/threat to appreciation. You went from leading with the more primitive part of your brain to your more reasoned part.

We have a choice about which brain phase runs our lives. We can't stop that initial fear response (as noted earlier). But we do have a choice in making a shift from living in threat to living in appreciation.

There are only two primary emotions: love and fear. All other emotions are secondary to these two. Anger is a secondary emotion, the outward expression of fear/threat. These emotional states of the limbic system are elicited by the lower reptilian (fear/threat) or higher neocortex (love/appreciation). The fear and threat happen automatically; we choose a shift to love and appreciation.

How We Disobey This Law

This particular Immutable Law is more about choices we fail to notice. Although we have lots of words and descriptions for emotions, they all are tied to the two primary emotions of fear/threat and love/appreciation. If we would rather not experience anger, resentment, regret, and jealousy, we need to shift away from the fear/threat mode. If we would rather experience joy, contentment, and connection, we must choose to move toward love/appreciation.

We disobey this law by not recognizing the origins of our emotional life (thoughts) and our choice in focusing on those thoughts. If we dwell on fearful thoughts, we activate and strengthen that brain phase. If we focus on appreciative thoughts, we activate and strengthen that brain phase. Since the more primitive parts of the brain automatically activate in protection mode, it is easy to slip into fear/threat. And many people then believe those thoughts to be more than just thoughts, but truth.

And we also disobey this law by constantly (although unintentionally) feeding our brain fear. This happens by constantly digesting fear-provoking images and words. For example, the news, both printed and broadcast, is specifically designed to activate fear. Fear is easy to elicit and difficult to turn off. Once we are hooked by fear, we will stay tuned. Staying tuned keeps us watching commercials. Commercials pay the profits of media outlets. We are hooked on fear, and they are hooked on profit. So, we watch as they serve fear. The same is true for much of popular music, hooking into our fear (mostly around love). It is also true for other media sources, often designed to elicit an us/them mentality. This mentality generally shifts us to fear. We fear "them," until we realize that the "them" is often manufactured.

As Maya Angelou reminded us, "We are more alike, my friends, than we are unalike."

How We Obey This Law

One major way of obeying this law is simply by understanding this particular dynamic of choice: fear/threat or love/appreciation. By understanding this, we can make new choices about where we spend our time and focus.

To be clear, this law is not about some emotions being bad and others being good. But it does seem that there are lower and higher emotions. I don't meet many people who want to be caught in the lower emotions associated with fear/threat (anger, resentment, regret, jealousy, and other related emotions). Most people would rather experience the higher emotions (joy, contentment, connection, and related emotions). They simply don't recognize how to shift away from the lower to the higher emotions.

A few days ago, I was meeting with a client who had spent her life struggling with depression. Her emotional life centered on anger and resentment. She also tended to see pending doom all around her. Daily news sent her into a fearful tailspin about where the world was heading.

Try as I might, she would not do any of the exercises I offered. So, I decided to share a little with her about her brain, her thoughts, and her emotions. When I finished, she sat in silence for a moment, thinking. And then, the anger sparked in her eyes, and she blurted, "So, you think it is just that easy, huh? Just 'shift my brain,' and everything will be OK. Well, it won't. My emotions are real. Not figments of my thoughts and brain. You can't just change that. I can't help it that bad things happen, and they happen to me. It's not my fault I feel the way I do. That's just the way I feel."

She finished, and I simply added, "No, I don't think it *is* that easy. But yes, I do think you can make a shift. And yes, I think it would shift your emotions. Not easy, but possible, depending on whether you understand it. I don't think you want to feel bad. I think that is why you are here. The question is really whether there is anything that can happen."

I paused for her to take a breath. Interestingly, I could see a shift in her right there, in that instant: the anger shifted. What she didn't recognize is that her brain had shifted, too.

She returned to her belief that emotions are real, attached to something important, and can't just shift.

So I asked, "So, where DO emotions come from? If not your thoughts, your mind, your brain, where?"

"They just are," she said. And then she pondered, "Wait, that can't be right. Otherwise, they are inconsequential. Okay, they are a result of things that happen, experiences."

I pushed, "So everyone has the same emotional response to the same event?"

"Sure..." She tried to be consistent. "Well, I think we have similar emotions about the same event."

"Really?" I questioned. "We had a recent election. Same experience. Some people are elated; others are devastated. Some are joyful, excited, and happy; others are sad, angry, worried. Same event—opposite ends of the emotional scale."

Being a news-watcher, she paused. "So, are you saying there is not a right reaction to that election? I mean, I think it is pretty clear what happened."

"Oh, I absolutely do not think there is a right reaction. Only reactions." I offered.

She questioned, "So, where did those reactions come from? I'm pretty sure my friends and I are right on this one. Our emotions were simply because we see what's happening."

An opening! I suggested, "Those having the opposite emotions as you and your friends also believe they see it clearly and correctly. In both cases, those thoughts about what is happening are triggering your emotions. Unfortunately, both sides can clearly validate their own thoughts. That doesn't make it true. It does demonstrate that the same circumstances can be seen from many perspectives." (Remember that earlier Law about Perspective?)

"But," she blurted, "there has to be a right perspective. Someone has to be right, and someone has to be wrong."

"Maybe," I offered, "but any argument is built on a set of underlying assumptions. You come to a conclusion based on your starting point. And another person comes to the opposite conclusion based on a different starting point. But my point is this: the same event elicited opposite emotions. Those emotions are based on the thoughts you had, not about what is right or wrong in society. Your thoughts about the event led to your emotions over the event."

My client agreed. But then she added, "So if someone has a 'lower' emotional response to the event, the person should just 'get with the program' and accept it?"

"Ah, great question," I responded. I explained that the point of this law is not that you have to have only a certain band of emotions. But simply that your brain can only function in one phase or another. We can only be in fear/threat or love/appreciation. It is up to each person to assess whether they want to be in that emotional state, and whether, from a little distance, it is justified.

Many people spend a lifetime feeling under threat, even though there is little outward evidence to support this. Some people with secure jobs are waiting for the pink slip. Some people with secure finances always feel that they are on the brink of bankruptcy. Some people with loving spouses are just waiting to be abandoned. Any of those things could, in the realm of reality, happen. The energy invested in the fear neither stops it from happening nor saves them from pain if it were to happen.

Since our brain is wired for threat/fear to be more automatic than love/appreciation, it is worth questioning one's current phase. If it is fear/threat, it is worth pondering whether that phase is warranted or not.

Which does raise the question: how do you make the shift?

It really is all about focus. Yes, that fear/threat area of your brain is pretty quickly and automatically activated. The question is how long it gets your attention. If you spend much of your life feeling threatened and fearful (indicated by spending much of your life in those lower emotional states), then you are focusing on those fearful/threatening thoughts.

Some event might trigger the brain's threat assessment. But the mind is where the focus is—thoughts. As we noted earlier in this book, thoughts are just that: thoughts. And we can choose, once aware, how tightly we hold to the thoughts. Or we can shift.

For just a moment, let's do a thought experiment. I am assuming, since you are reading this, you are at this moment in a safe place. Usually, we don't spend much time reading in high-risk situations. I'm assuming you are not hanging out in a dark and dangerous alley right now or sitting at the watering hole on the savannah with lions to your back. If I am wrong, your fear phase is already activated.

So, for just a moment, recall a fearful experience in the last few weeks. Don't go with a really big one in life, just a point when you felt fearful. Perhaps a moment in traffic or at work. Something that made you fearful, but maybe not terrified. Think about that incident for a moment before you continue reading.

Okay, I'm assuming you followed through and probably felt the fear grip you. It might have spiked your blood pressure a little, perhaps caused you to breathe a bit heavier. And your muscles probably tensed. In essence, your body was preparing for defense. It was getting you ready for a physical altercation, if necessary.

Notice that nothing actually changed in your immediate environment. The change was entirely internal. It started with a remembered moment of threat and quickly became a physical response. Your brain's threat center went on alert when you were remembering, and your body followed.

Let's make a switch. For a moment, think about a time when you were loving life. Maybe it was a wonderful moment with family or friends. Perhaps it was a time you were helping someone in need. Or it may be that special place that is beautiful and serene for you. Just spend a moment or two picturing it, imagining it, thinking about how it smelled and felt. Linger in that moment before you come back to the book.

Again, I am assuming you followed through on that. Once that fear response has kicked in, it might take a moment or two to shift. But, you probably noticed your spirits lift. Your body probably relaxed, your breathing likely shifted down to that belly breathing, perhaps a little joy broke through.

Nothing external changed. Same environment, same circumstances. The only shift was in your thinking. But, your thinking shifted your brain phase. Your threat zone reduced its threat assessment. Your appreciation zone kicked in and took control.

And now you know: it is possible that nothing in your environment changes, but your emotional state can shift—in either direction. No real threat has to be present to act as if there is a threat. And conversely, you can also choose love/appreciation at any time.

You can either live in threat/fear or love/appreciation. Your brain can't be in both phases at the same time. And now, you have a choice in which area you live.

There are times when your environment actually triggers that threat/fear. There is nothing wrong with our brain alerting us to a threat or danger. If we **are** in danger, that is how we survive. If we are not in danger, but constantly live in fear, we stay miserable.

The preponderance of times when we feel that threat and fear, there is no real danger. Yet our brain stays locked in perceived danger or is simply overloaded by fear.

Now, it becomes your choice. Do you stay stuck in fear/threat or do you make a shift to love/appreciation? (To learn more about using appreciation and gratitude, here is some additional training: http://thriveology.com/appreciation)

CHAPTER 16

We Are Built for Impact

The ancient philosophers believed that everything has an innate purpose. Each part of nature has a purpose for itself—not a purpose to serve people, but for itself (so, yes, even mosquitoes have their own purpose, even if I don't like their purpose).

Trees are designed to grow leaves, fruit, and nuts. A tree that does not produce leaves will not make it long. If it does not make fruit or nuts, the tree species will not survive.

Animals also do what they are designed to do, following their instincts and inborn tendencies. They follow their design in the world—or they perish.

I believe humans have an inborn design, too. It's a bit different than the rest of wildlife, because we get to choose how we carry it out.

How do we find that design? There are some pretty clear signs out there.

Study after study shows that life satisfaction is more tied to altruism and making a difference than anything else. Studies also show that *giving* creates much more joy and satisfaction than *getting*.

Volunteer and charity work has long been shown to raise levels of joy, happiness, and life satisfaction. At the same time, self-focus and self-centered activity lead to lower levels of life satisfaction. People on a path of self-satisfaction discover there is never enough money or "fun" to keep them happy. Momentary spikes of adrenaline-fueled excitement are followed by a craving for more. It's like grabbing that carb-laden, sweet-tasting snack for a jolt of energy, only to have a sugar crash and a craving for more.

Humans, I believe, are designed for impact. Our inborn design is to make a difference in the world around us. And when we aren't doing that, we retreat into distraction and addiction.

To clarify *impact:* our actions and decisions affect other people. They make an impact. It is like throwing a rock into a still pond. Those ripples start at the point of impact and move outward—not one ripple, but multiple ripples. Since we are all doing that, it is more like a multitude of multiple ripples—an ocean full—moving through the world.

We will make an impact. That's unavoidable. But the impact can be good or bad, intentional or unintentional. So the question of importance is whether you are making a positive or negative impact and whether it is done intentionally or unintentionally.

Let's take an example we all experienced in life: parenting. You were parented by someone in a specific way. And you are likely, statistically speaking, to parent one or more people. I think we can readily agree that not all parenting is good. In fact, some parenting is downright bad and hurtful. And, it makes an impact. We can viscerally know that parenting is important (if not crucial) for development. But in the moments of parenting, sometimes the actions are counterproductive to healthy development. Parents often lose track of the effect they are having.

People who parent in unhealthy ways often were parented in unhealthy ways. They are just doing what was done to them. (Yes, there can be other reasons, but this is the primary reason.) They were impacted by bad parenting, and their children will be impacted by that impact. The ripple of bad parenting moves through multiple generations.

Then there are those who parent in healthy ways. Their children are much more likely to parent in healthy ways—and this ripple also moves through multiple generations.

Here is the crucial part: anyone at any time can decide to change actions. If someone was parented unhealthily, that person can choose another path—intentionally changing the type of impact made. Either way, there is an impact.

As a therapist, I have spent hours and hours with clients trying to heal and move through painful moments of dysfunctional childhoods. Some of the healing often included realizing their parents did not mean to cause harm—they were also struggling with pain from their childhood. The ripple effect. Impact.

One client, "Christie," told me about her neglectful and hurtful childhood. Much of her pain came from feeling unloved and unprotected by her mother. Her father left the family when Christie was very young. And her mother was emotionally distant from Christie, unable to provide nurture or care. Christie only saw her father on rare occasions and shared little emotional bond.

As Christie grew up, she struggled with friends and school. Christie often reacted angrily to her teachers. And she admits she was always jealous of her friends with loving parents. Christie shifted between anger and depression through much of her adolescence. She retreated into unhealthy relationships with boys, desperate to have any attention. This led to drinking and drugs.

But somehow Christie, with no help from her family, made it into college. Her first few years of college were hazy, filled more with parties and dates than classes. During her sophomore year, Christie ended up on academic probation. The administration let her know that if her grades did not change, she would be headed home.

Christie told me that was the only inspiration she needed. There was no way she wanted to return home. She thought of her family life and had no desire to return to it. So, she buckled down, cut back on partying, and pulled her grades up. During that time, she met someone. He showed Christie attention, treated her well, and was funny. Christie, not used to being treated well, was confused and excited. She didn't believe she deserved love. And she began to realize how hurt she had been throughout her life.

During their courtship, Christie began to realize her feelings of inadequacy and insecurity had less to do with herself and more to do with how she had been parented. It was then that Christie realized she was living out what she had been parented into believing. Christie felt unloved and made sure she was unlovable. Christie felt insecure and created insecure relationships. Christie felt damaged and formed damaging relationships.

This moment of clarity was enough. During the next couple of years, Christie turned herself around. She dove into her classes and student government. She fell in love. And she got a good job.

A year later, Christie got married. She and her husband were doing great. They were loving and respectful of each other—until their first child. At that point, something shifted inside for Christie. She didn't have a model for good parenting, so she began to automatically use the model of parenting she did have. Christie's husband watched his loving wife become a bitter and angry mother. Their marriage began to deteriorate.

Two years into parenthood, Christie angrily told her husband to "get out," after he once more tried to keep her from yelling at their child. Her husband did what he had refused to do the other times this had happened. He left. And Christie suddenly had a moment of clarity. She was watching her husband walk out the door at the same point in her child's life when Christie's father walked out of hers. Christie wondered, "Did my father want to leave, or did he have to leave?" Never before had it crossed her mind that her father might have loved her, might have wanted to stay, but had given up.

Christie looked down at her child, sitting on the floor and crying over the conflict. Christie saw herself. She saw how desperately she needed love, needed nurture. She needed a hug. Christie's heart melted. She scooped up her child and held her tight. Christie called her husband, begging him to come home. He agreed with one stipulation: Christie had to go to therapy. She readily agreed.

Which is how she ended up in my office.

In the moment of staring at her crying child, Christie got it. That child was entirely innocent. All those frustrating moments were not about a child trying to "drive her crazy." It was just a child being a child—just like Christie had been.

We spent some time talking about her childhood. Christie grieved the parenting she never had. She grieved the time she let slip between her fingers, angry and lashing out. And she grieved the hurt she had caused her husband and her child.

Then, Christie committed to changing who she was and how she acted in the world. During this time, she felt it necessary to reach out to family and friends, apologizing for the hurt she had caused. She contacted several people she had dragged into her partying lifestyle. It was tough, and not entirely her responsibility, but she wanted to apologize. Christie realized that even while she thought herself insignificant and worthless, she had impacted people around her.

And Christie decided that going forward, she wanted her impact to be positive. This decision led her to relearn parenting and to rebuild her marriage. She became interested in helping others, went back to school, and became a family therapist. She decided she wanted to help heal other families, hoping to keep others from experiencing the pain she had felt. Christie now makes an impact, positively and intentionally.

Throughout our lives, we impact other people. Sometimes, the impact is for the better. Sometimes, it is harmful. The question is whether we can become intentional about the impact—can we *choose* to make an impact for the better?

(You may be wondering if there are people who choose to make an impact for the worst. The answer is yes. We humans often work from pain or justification. We choose to be hurtful because of our own hurt. Or we choose to justify behavior that is often greed, in the mistaken belief that this will lead to happiness.)

How We Disobey This Law

Humans cannot help but impact others. Whether positive or negative, we make an impact. Perhaps you can think of people in your own life who have pulled you away from more positive aspects of living? In school, "peer pressure" was a constant topic. While peer pressure always originates from a place of internal insecurity, there are those who pull toward the negative—not just in grade school, but throughout life. Whether we respond to their impact or not is up to us. But pull they will.

More and more, I am convinced that their reason is not to have people around them become unhealthy, as much as it is a desire to have others at their level. In some ways, it justifies their own "unhealth," if others exist there, too. Inadvertently, they have a negative impact.

You can't help but make an impact. The question is what type of impact you will have and how you feel about that impact. Remember, our design is to make an impact. And I also believe that when we are not consciously making a positive impact, we know it.

If we are not following our internal design, we often seek out some replacement feeling. I believe many of our struggles with addiction and distraction are based on not intentionally following a life of impact. When we disobey this law, we are not intentional about the impact we are making. When we are not intentional, we shift away from our design and look for distractions. Addiction is the primary way we stay distracted. Drugs and alcohol are not our only ways. Any attempt to numb and distract can become an addiction as we seek more and more ways to avoid the pain of not living our design.

That does not mean that people who make a positive impact might not struggle with addiction/distraction. It might be worth noting, though, that addiction recovery includes a shift to positive impact. The process is not merely about stopping the addictive behavior, but of finding a better way of living. Often, the primary aspect is about seeking forgiveness and making a difference, such as helping others who struggle with addiction. But that makes a very different ripple of impact than participating in addiction with others.

We WILL have an impact. It is up to us to decide if the impact is positive or negative.

How We Obey This Law

When we recognize we make an impact, and when we consciously decide the type of impact we want to make, we obey this law.

Humans cannot help but make an impact. When we look around at our planet, we see our footprint everywhere. Cities have sprouted up. Farms have cut through the earth. Jungles have been tamed. Inhospitable areas are inhabited. Mountains are conquered. Seas are farmed. Human impact is impossible to avoid or deny. That impact is caused by individuals. By you.

We can see the impact and recognize that the impact has both good and bad aspects. We can't miss seeing the incessant impact we make.

And humans do impact each other, both in positive and negative ways. Reflect back on your day and note the places where YOU made an impact. Interestingly, most people spend time thinking about their day in terms of how others have impacted THEM. We don't spend much time pondering how we impact others. This is why we are far less intentional about our impact than we should be.

In my grade school years, I was clear on when someone hurt my feelings or treated me poorly. I was aware of when others had been kind to me, impacting me in positive ways. But I remember one day in fifth grade when another student told me I had hurt her feelings. She told me that my words had been hurtful.

A friend and I had been teasing. We were not kind, but I wasn't noticing that. I missed the fact that I might be impacting her in a negative way.

When she confronted me, I remember feeling embarrassed. But I also remember realizing that I could either be a negative influence or a positive one. I had, at that point, chosen negative.

I wish I could tell you that this fifth-grade experience sent me on a life of only being positive and making a positive impact. That would be a lie. I did become more aware of how my words could help or harm. I did become aware I had more power than I recognized. I did become aware that I could do harm, even if I didn't mean to do harm.

I know that I have hurt others. I know I have been a negative impactor on my world and on other people. Making an impact is inevitable. The question is whether we are conscious of this and work to choose our impact.

There will be those who choose to make a negative impact. But over the years, I have become more and more convinced that most people want to make a positive impact. There are also times when a positive impact in one direction causes a negative impact in another direction. People tend to note their positive impact and ignore the negative. Any action, as physics reminds us, has consequences. If we cannot help but make an impact, our task is to aim that impact in a positive direction.

One note: While there can be both positive and negative impacts to many of our actions, this is not true with relationships. Having a positive impact upon someone has little potential for a negative impact, too. Having a positive impact as a parent has little potential for negative impact. Having a positive impact as a friend, boss, colleague, or any other role has little potential for creating a negative impact. We can always be a positive impactor in relationships!

HOW TO CHOOSE YOUR IMPACT

I believe people are designed to impact. And I also believe that people have a deep desire to make a positive impact. Unfortunately, this sometimes gets lost in the tugs and pulls of life. While we are designed for impact, the world often discourages it. This leaves a deep yearning within us, yet few answers on why. That yearning is, I believe, calling us back to being a positive impact.

Since those impact muscles may be a bit weak, it can be helpful to have a checklist as you ponder how to be of more impact. In essence, this is about consciously choosing your point of impact, choosing a life of impact.

1) Passion: When John came into my office, it appeared that any "life" had been squeezed out of him. John told me he couldn't remember the last time he looked forward to the day. It was just a matter of dragging himself through the day, waiting for it to end.

After several sessions, it became clear that John was out of touch with passion. I could tell because when I asked what John would love to do, his eyes lit up; he sat up straight and started telling me about his concerns for our youth. He told me he felt that the inner city had such potential, but was untapped. He saw it every day when he arrived at his company, a warehouse in a poorer section of the city.

John told me that every drive into work broke his heart as he saw the youth milling around, often missing school, falling into drugs and gangs. It haunted John.

So, I asked what John would do if he could. He told me the youth needed a chance. Even if only a handful took it, he felt they needed a chance. And then he described his dream of a private boarding school. He told me education was key, but so were different surroundings, as an insulation from the negative influences.

John was passionate. I pushed John to have some discussions with friends. He did. Given his success, John had access to people with resources. And given his passion, he was contagious. An old building in the poorest section of his town is now a boarding school. Families are included in the process, but John is devoted to finding students who want something different and helping them get there. John's passion has impacted many people: the students and families involved, but also the supporters and volunteers.

Tapping into passions to make a difference is the first step to being a positive impact.

2) Gifts and Talents: Your impact is in your design. And so are your gifts, talents, and abilities. Some will argue you are born with those gifts; others will argue you develop them through early experiences. I argue that it doesn't matter; what matters is using them.

What good is a talent or gift you have if it is not applied—and applied for the greater good?

You are gifted. But you may not know it. For many, gifts fall into the area of, "That's just what I do." It seems so normal to you that you may miss it. You may not even acknowledge it as a talent or gift.

A while back, I took the StrengthsFinder assessment by Gallup. To be honest, I have taken a myriad of tests and assessments over the course of my life and career. Some were intended to weed candidates out of processes. Others were meant to help in the assessment of myself, either for my or other's information. So, I am used to the tests and the subsequent result reports.

If you are not familiar, the StrengthsFinder assessment is based on the understanding that there are 34 core strengths humans can possess. The goal of the test is to help you identify your top strengths—not so you know about all the things you need to fix, but so you know how to function from your strengths more and more.

When I was younger, there seemed to be a prevailing notion that you needed to shore up all your weak areas. Not good here? Work on it. Not good there? Work on it.

We now know people are happier, more engaged, and more productive when they are working from their strengths. StrengthsFinder is designed to help you identify and claim your strengths. (Learn more about this test here: http://thriveology.com/strength)

Which is my point here: you probably don't know what your strengths and abilities are unless you have had some help in identifying them.

After I took the assessment, I remember having a reaction I have had to similar tests in the past, "So, not everyone does things this way? Not everyone naturally does these things?" At that point, it would be wise for me to understand that any impact I make will likely come from within my strengths, my gifts and talents, my abilities.

I am not a great mathematician; it is extremely unlikely I will make any contribution in the area of theoretical (or even applied) physics. It is not within my scope of gifts (nor particularly in the realm of my passions). I am not a skilled athlete; it is very unlikely I will make an impact in the realm of athletic endeavors. I am not a skilled jurist; it is highly unlikely I will make an impact in the legal world.

To be clear, that does not mean I might not enjoy those areas. I have an interest in cosmology and have always loved looking at the night sky. I hope to always be running trails and paddling waterways. And I follow politics to see where the world is turning.

But my impact will come from my own talents, gifts, and abilities. It is just what I do more naturally and automatically.

As I have already stated, many people don't really know their talents, skills, and abilities. They don't know their unique "ability-print." If that is you, there are a few tried-and-true ways of assessing:

WATCH: Notice yourself. What do you naturally like to do? How do you naturally see the world? How do you interact with the world differently than those around you?

ASK: Inquire with friends and family. Ask them to give you some insight into your gifts. What is it they see you do that is different than others—that is uniquely you? My guess is you can name the gifts and talents of your close friends. This is because it is easier to see these things from the outside. Inside, you see it as "just you." Likewise, others see the talent in you, so ask.

TEST: Take an assessment. While I have no connection to the company, I think the StrengthsFinder assessment is an excellent tool to discover and access your talents and gifts. But there are others.

Once you are clear about your strengths, talents, and gifts, you know your impact will likely come from applying them, through your passion, to where the world needs a difference.

3) Integrity: Making a positive impact always comes from a place of integrity. In fact, if you find yourself out of integrity, you can bet you are not at a place of positive impact. Those moments when you trade your integrity for anything are the moments that the shift is toward what you can get, not what you can give. Impact, at least positive impact, always comes from giving (see *Service* below).

Many times, integrity is tested by others who see an opportunity inherent in the impact you make. You might start at a point of positive impact, only to have someone else see an opportunity and push away from impact into exploitation. You will have to make the choice of integrity.

Let me be clear: There are plenty of people and organizations that do well by doing good. Many companies find opportunities that are both profitable and make a positive impact. Many professionals make a positive impact while still making a living. There is a line, though, between impact and exploit.

As I have spent time with professionals and entrepreneurs, when this question comes up, I always suggest a "gut check." Usually, when I am having this conversation, it is self-selected to those who really want to make a positive impact. Opportunists who are only focused on "getting" have already been weeded out. They don't seek help in how to be a positive impact.

Those with whom I coach and consult want to make a positive impact. So, a "gut check" simply ties them back to their own place of integrity. The gut check is not about whether they deserve to make a living (I assume that), but whether they have stayed on the side of impact without crossing into exploitation.

Generally, companies start out impact-agnostic. They are neutral on how they move forward. Some companies solely focus on profit, at all costs. And integrity is one of the costs. Others choose to serve their customer well, doing good in the world, while still being profitable. Integrity is part of the fabric of the company.

Professionals have the same questions to ask. I know of two CPA's. One sees it as her role to protect her clients while helping them see opportunities for saving money or gaining profit. She does her job with the highest level of integrity. The other CPA works hard to help his clients hide their money from scrutiny. Doing so might be seen as being of service to his clients. But his integrity was compromised long ago. The net effect is a negative impact. His clients continue legally dubious actions, governmental agencies are duped, and this CPA had to give up his integrity years ago.

My guess, if you are reading to this point, is you are committed to being a positive impact. Consult your integrity. If you are outside of integrity, this is a sign that you are missing the positive impact point. You will not consistently make a positive impact if you are out of your bounds of integrity.

4) Potentiality: Being of positive impact pulls people to higher potential. It calls to aspiration and hope. We are all caught somewhere between *lack* and *potential*. When caught in lack, we focus on what we don't have, what isn't possible, and what can't be. It creates a strong trap of hopelessness.

Potential taps into resources, aspirations, hopes, dreams, and possibilities. It opens the path and frees people. Potential opens the world; lack closes the doors.

Positive impact is always based in potentiality. It taps into an energy of what could be, opening the path to a better place and world than was there before.

In physics, an object has potential energy in it. This energy is stored for release, depending on the forces acting upon it and the closeness of other objects. In other words, the potential energy has to be activated. It is there but awaiting some action.

Impact comes from the release of the potential. When we positively impact someone, it frees up their potential. It also frees the potential of the impactor. When we are not impactors, we stagnate. When we are creating a positive impact, we generate energy, and release it, causing the person impacted to more easily tap into their potential. For example:

- A child who is fed can access their potential more easily than when the child was starving.
- A previously homeless person can express more potential when housed than when on the street.
- A struggling student who receives tutoring can express potential that was previously trapped by a lack of knowledge or understanding.
- A rescued dog can express the potential for being a wonderful companion better than when the dog was at risk.

Positive impact taps into the potential of the impactor and the impacted. The potential was already there. A positive impact builds and releases the innate potential.

5) Love: Impact comes from love. Not the romantic feeling we call "love," but the action of showing love. That action always comes from within and moves toward another person. This love is based on compassion and giving. It stands in contrast to negative impact, which originates in greed and getting. Love and greed both create impact. The difference is in the flow. Is it outward or inward? Toward others or away from others? Positive impact or negative impact?

I have a deep love for bodies of water. Perhaps my own internal representation of impact as the ripples on a pond, caused by the impact point of a pebble, comes from that love. I enjoy swimming, diving, paddling, and just about any other activity on or in the water. When I stand in the ocean, I often find myself just moving my arms through the water to feel the sensation and see the effect on the water. If I push my arm away from my chest and outward, the wave moves outward, away from me. If I stretch my arm out from my side and draw it toward my chest, I pull the water toward me.

With my impact, am I "making waves" outward toward others, or drawing them to myself?

If impact is about giving, focused on moving your resources outward, it will likely be positive. If it is about getting, focused on pulling resources inward, it will likely be negative.

Interestingly, you might notice that with my analogy of water and waves, either way, the water returns to a normal level. When we focus on compassion and giving, there is always more. When we focus on greed and getting, it rarely lasts too long—and never lasts forever. When we move outward, the ripple keeps moving, further and further away.

6) Service: Related to love is service. Positive impact comes from asking, "How can I serve?" Leaders who focus on being of service find willing followers. Leaders who focus on having power have few or reluctant followers. Service is always based on the need of others.

Any individual or company has the capacity to be of service. A company can commit to making the best product that provides for a need. For example, if building a smartphone, making it the best, user-friendly, reliable device is acting from a place of service. However, making the cheapest, but most profitable device, which may or may not be useful in a time of need, is not. Based on service or self-service?

Power is a tricky issue in all our lives. Parents often believe they "should" just be respected and given power. But parenting is entirely about service. How can you best serve that child (the one you brought into the world) so that the child grows into a person of positive impact? (This is not the same as losing yourself in the parenting role; it is about seeing the service involved in the role.)

Many companies have made the mistake of believing that customers somehow owe them for being their customer. Those companies have lost sight of serving the customer, often even being resentful when customers interact with them.

Many politicians lose sight with the fact they have been chosen to serve. They have not been given power for power's sake. At their best, politicians seek to serve their constituents. They move from the point of service, not power. This creates a space of respect, not contempt, on both sides.

Politicians of service build power in their efforts to make a difference in the world. Politicians of power seize opportunities for their own benefit, often to the detriment of the world. The difference is between offering service and seizing power. And that changes the outcome of their impact.

Those who seek to serve are entrusted with power. Those who seek power often find themselves mistrusted and disliked. More than that, those seeking power often create a negative impact in their efforts to gather power. And those who seek to serve often create a positive impact in their efforts to serve.

7) Stretch: Making an impact—the real impact of which you are capable— will stretch you. When we move into those places that call upon our talents and passions, when we are rising to our highest integrity and releasing our potential, when we are of service in love, we are stretched to new places. Our capacity for growth will catch up quickly as we are stretched more and more.

Every real impact starts with a stretch into new space. Being of impact calls us to places we have never been in ways we have never been.

It can be uncomfortable. New ways of action always leave us a bit uncomfortable, but that can be a clear indication you are shifting. In fact, unless there is a bit of discomfort, you are likely at the same place you were before. Growth and change are accompanied by discomfort and frustration. Be assured that the discomfort is temporary while you are growing into the new space and becoming "just who you are."

You are designed for impact. Make it a positive impact. One that stretches you and challenges you. It will impact you, as well as the world around you. You will be living your design!

CHAPTER 17

Don't Fight the Laws—
Follow Them:
A Life of Impact

I t is my hope you have had a number of reactions to these Immutable Laws of Living. I hope there were occasions when you said, "Of course, that's obvious." At other times, I hope you thought, "That matches my experience, I just hadn't put it into words." At still other times, I hope you murmured, "I'm not sure about that; I need to think it through." And I do hope there were times when you absolutely challenged me and thought, "This guy is WAY wrong!" If you thought that, I would just ask you to try it out. Test the law—not by breaking it, but by following it. See if it helps to follow and obey the law.

AFTER you have tested it, to see if I am right (versus just believing I am wrong), if the law doesn't hold together, please let me know. Drop me an email (Lee@Thriveology.com) and share your experience. That way I can think and test some more.

If it occurs to you that I missed an Immutable Law, please let me know that, too. I have the same limits of thinking as anyone. The laws in this book are the ones that have worked for me and have held true for my clients. That doesn't mean there aren't others.

So, what now?

Here's a little secret: If you follow that last law, almost all the others will simply fall into place. It's kind of like choosing to drive safely in a car. If you are driving safely, you are likely obeying all the laws just by the nature of being safe.

If you live a life of impact, the other laws get covered, even if they seem a bit unrelated. (Remember, there is an interconnectedness in all the laws anyway.) Many of the laws are broken because of one simple reason: we are not living our design. We are not living the impact for which we are designed.

When we aren't living a life of impact, life seems unfair. We try to make it about happiness. Challenges seem like dead-ends. We duck our own responsibility, believing every thought that pops into our minds. Our perspective is never challenged or stretched. We see people for their issues, not their innocence. We fight change. Fears limit us at every turn. We struggle to accept what life brings us, and try desperately to control things over which we have no control. We don't live in the present, preferring to dwell on the past or anxiously await the future. We waste time, living in fear. We don't find our place of meaning and purpose.

OR, we pursue a life of impact.

YOU matter to the world. You have something to do, some mission to live. It is in your design. It is simply waiting for you to choose. Find your purpose, tap into your power, and live your passion.

Don't wait for life to happen. Choose to live a life of impact. The world is waiting.

A LIST OF THE IMMUTABLE LAWS OF LIVING

Life Is Not Fair
Life Has Challenges
Life Isn't About Happiness
Thoughts Are Just Thoughts
Every Perspective Is Limited
Change Is Inevitable
People Do the Best They Can
We All Have Fears
Your Life is YOUR Responsibility
What Is IS What Is
Control What You Can and Release the Rest
Forgive to Fully Live
Life Is In the NOW
Time Is Our Most Precious Commodity
We Live In Fear or Love
We Are Built for Impact

ABOUT THE AUTHOR

Dr. Lee Baucom is a coach, consultant, therapist, author, and frequent speaker. In his work, Dr. Baucom strives to help individuals, couples, families, businesses, and organizations to thrive. For several decades, Dr. Baucom has helped individuals transform their lives and thrive.

The author of a number of books, including *Thrive Principles*, *The Forgive Process*, and *How To Save Your Marriage In 3 Simple Steps*, Dr. Baucom provides practical steps to create a thriving life.

You can learn more about the Thrive Principles at http://TheThrivePrinciples.com

If you would like to contact Dr. Baucom for coaching, consulting, or speaking, you can contact him here:

Aspire Coaching
4949 Brownsboro Rd., #147
Louisville, Kentucky 40222
502-802-4823
Lee@Thriveology.com

Morgan James
Speakers Group

↗ www.TheMorganJamesSpeakersGroup.com

We connect Morgan James published
authors with live and online events
and audiences who will benefit
from their expertise.

Morgan James makes all of our titles available
through the Library for All Charity Organization.

www.LibraryForAll.org

Printed in the USA
CPSIA information can be obtained
at www.ICGtesting.com
JSHW022354190224
57682JS00005B/474